Adjusting the numbers: The future of finance in law firms

EDITED BY ALEX DAVIES

Commissioning editor
Alex Davies

Published by
Globe Law and Business Ltd
3 Mylor Close
Horsell
Woking
Surrey GU21 4DD
United Kingdom
Tel: +44 20 3745 4770
www.globelawandbusiness.com

ISBN: 978-1-78358-404-8
A catalogue record for this book is available from the British Library

Contents

Executive summary

We began 2020 in bright spirits and bountiful economic conditions; by early March all that had changed. Economic adjustments were made and, overall, firms ended the year in much better shape than their spring worst-case projections anticipated. Some firms were even close to their original 2020 profit expectations to date – largely due to quick actions to curtail expenditures as COVID-19 got underway in the US.

Our opening chapter, by James D. Cotterman of Altman Weil, looks back at a year like no other in our lifetimes, identifying good compensation practices that can be applied during the pandemic, its gradual cessation, and beyond.

Pricing lessons from the previous global financial crisis, a little over a decade ago, have proven extremely pertinent today for the legal sector. Although the current cause, magnitude, and environment today differs (sometimes dramatically), we would do well to heed General George S. Patton when he stated, "prepare for the unknown by studying how others in the past have coped with the unforeseeable and the unpredictable".

As any good pricing practitioner will tell you, the approach to good pricing should not fundamentally change in an economic downturn as the majority of the same key principles still apply. But what are these principles, how should we best be responding to client needs both now and post-pandemic, and how do we ensure that our businesses also remain successful, profitable, and viable in the longer term? Chapter two, by Stuart Dodds of Positive Pricing, provides an overview of the key themes law firms should consider when looking at pricing through today's lens, gives insights to what other leading law firms are doing to protect their pricing position, and suggests a roadmap for the immediate, mid- and longer-term.

Law firms tend to lack performance management systems for shareholders. Indeed, too often the requirement to become a shareholder is demonstrating significant competence as an associate, which is a very different role. Shareholders should not simply be considered more senior associates, with higher billing rates, and possibly, but not always, the ability to generate new business. Shareholders have an obligation to act in the best interests of the firm, in both the short- and long-term. Law firm owners must devote time and energy to pursuits beyond lawyering, such as training, mentoring, recruiting, supervising, managing matters, managing people, managing clients, representing the firm in the public eye, and generating new business. In most firms, almost none of this is recognized, tracked, or rewarded. As law firms adjust to a rapidly changing marketplace, the role of shareholder is evolving as well. Chapter three by Tim Corcoran discusses what it means to become, and remain, a shareholder in the law firm of tomorrow.

Chapter four, by Mary Juetten of Traklight, begins with some bold overarching statements:

- Most lawyers do not understand that they are running a business;
- Many lawyers do not like numbers, yet still try to set pricing for their services;
- Most lawyers do not budget or estimate billings or costs for a case; and
- Many firms, of all sizes, set billing rates and compensation based solely on the market.

This year has been tough to say the least, but does not change the fundamentals of running a law practice, from solo to Big Law. For many, it has now become essential to understand the data required to measure performance and critical to budget, price, and predict revenue. Like we tell our clients, Mary says, seek professional help with business aspects, but be informed so to protect your practice, regardless of size.

Prior to COVID-19, ask any law firm managing partner or CFO to honestly tell you what their firm's primary existential priorities were and they would probably say, "Increasing profitability and market share, investing in the right people and technology and maintaining and attracting new clients". Things like technological innovation, business optimization, process transformation, information security, relationship management, service delivery effectiveness have also been important, but for many firms these initiatives were secondary, strategic components that took a back seat to maintaining profitability in the face of hyper-competitiveness. COVID-19 not only has acerbated an already hyper-competitive legal marketplace, but it has changed the dynamics of legal competitiveness and perhaps forever changed the delivery of legal services model by moving all of those strategies into the driver's seat as the world has become increasingly virtual and digitized.

As we hopefully move past the pandemic and into the new legal marketplace, law firms are on the cusp of making an important decision as they prepare to resume business: Do we go back to *business as usual* or embrace all of the *advancements and efficiencies* brought on by COVID-19? It is a pivotable moment for many firms and important enough to shape their destiny and impact their profitability. The answer is easy and evidenced all around us by how countless businesses have transformed themselves, adapted to change, and advanced their business transformation at lightning speed all in order to service their clients. In the new legal marketplace, change and innovation is no longer just an option, it is an absolute necessity for those firms that want to be profitable and quite simply exist in a post-COVID marketplace. It is no longer just about the law, but just as importantly about the business, value, and delivery of the law. Clinging to the past is not an option. In chapter five, Richard Brzakala looks at how COVID-19 has impacted the legal marketplace, competitiveness, service delivery, and client expectations facing law firms in the new legal marketplace.

In chapter six, Andrew O'Connor and Louis Young from Augusta Ventures look at options for law firm financing in difficult times, and how litigation finance can mitigate risk. The chapter summarizes the five typical financing options available to law firms and gives an overview of litigation finance as a risk-free option. The authors deep dive into the mechanics of how litigation finance works and discuss the commercial models for utilising litigation financing.

Chapter seven by Andy Poole discusses how law firms have historically managed their practices and finances and the traditional drivers of profitability and cash generation, before examining the impact of COVID-19 on the performance and finances of law firms and the financial lessons to be learned from the experience. The chapter references the implications of and impacts on working from home/flexibly, the need for and use of technology, office environments (or lack thereof), outsourcing, the rise of virtual/platform firms, and compensation, rewards, and incentives for staff and partners, discussing how all will dictate the finances of the future law firm.

About the authors

Richard Brzakala is a recognized legal marketplace thought leader and expert in legal operations, sourcing, and cost efficiency strategies. He has been a trusted advisor to many senior executives and general counsels, having worked and consulted for numerous FIs, law firms, and government agencies. Richard is a frequent speaker, panelist, and writer, having published numerous articles on a variety of legal ops topics such as legal sourcing, winning RFPs, convergence practices, and creating corporate cost-saving strategies. Richard is the author of *Show Me The Math: The Importance of Cost Estimates When Engaging A Law Firm*,a contributing author for Thomson Reuters Legal Executive Institute, and also participates in an executive advisory capacity for a number of global IT legal service providers. In 2017, a leading US publication recognized and awarded Richard with its annual Trailblazers award for his work in developing a comprehensive global methodology for evaluating law firm compliance with cyber security standards. Richard is currently working as the global director of external legal services at a large FI in Canada where his mandate includes the oversite of legal ops, compliance, finance, and risk management practices as they relate to the management of external counsel globally.

Timothy B. Corcoran is principal of Corcoran Consulting Group, a trustee and fellow of the College of Law Practice Management, past president and Hall of Fame member of the Legal Marketing Association, an American Lawyer Fellow, and a teaching fellow in the Master of Legal Business program at the Australian College of Law. A former CEO, Tim advises law firm and law department leaders through the profitable disruption of outdated business models.

James D. Cotterman is a principal with Altman Weil, Inc. He advises law firms on compensation, capital structure, and other economic issues, governance, management, and law firm merger assessments. Before joining Altman Weil in 1988, James was manager of acquisitions for a public company in the health care industry, where he developed, evaluated, negotiated, and integrated merger opportunities.

James is the author of *Cotterman on Compensation*, a blog on lawyer compensation and law firm finance. He is the lead author of the ABA's *Compensation Plans for Law Firms* and is a member of the Board of Editors of Accounting and Financial Planning for Law Firms. His writings have appeared in *The American Lawyer, The National Law Journal*, ABA's *Law Practice, International Law Firm Management* and many other publications.

James is a frequent speaker and lecturer including presentations for annual and regional conferences of the American Bar Association and the Association of Legal Administrators, as well as numerous state and local Bar and ALA meetings. He is a Fellow of the College of Law Practice Management. Academic credentials include an undergraduate degree in Operations Management and an MBA in Accounting, both from Syracuse University. James is a licensed certified public accountant in the Commonwealth of Pennsylvania and is a member of the American and Pennsylvania Institutes of Certified Public Accountants.

Stuart Dodds is co-founder and principal of Positive Pricing, a professional services-focused pricing consulting firm, and board member of the Legal Value Network. With nearly 30 years' professional service and law firm experience he was one of the first and longest serving legal pricing and legal project management directors in the industry and is the author of *Smarter Pricing, Smarter Profit*, one of the first books covering law firm pricing, negotiation, and LPM, published by the American Bar Association.

Mary Juetten, the author of *Small Law Firm KPIs: How to Measure your Way to Greater Profits* and *The Business of Legal: The Data-Driven Law Practice*, plus founder and CEO of Traklight, has dedicated her more-than-35-year career to helping businesses achieve and protect their success. Mary is a professional accountant, attorney, and mediator and recently trained in collaborative law. Specializing in leading companies in transition or start-up phases and helping them create sustainable, operational, and financial growth, Mary wants entrepreneurs and businesses to have Fortune 500 style software solutions. Using her extensive education, including a Bachelor of Commerce degree from McGill and a Juris Doctorate and Master of Law from Arizona State, as well as her US and Canadian accounting and public accountant certifications, Mary created the only self-guided software platform that creates a custom intellectual property (IP) strategy plus assesses business risk. Traklight

Pro acts as lead generation or triage for companies, business, start-up and venture, and IP attorneys, CPAs, and other professionals. Mary is an international author, blogger, speaker, and mentor. She previously represented entrepreneurs on the Board of the Crowdfunding Investment Regulatory Advocates and the Emerging Enterprise Committee of the Licensing Executives Society. In 2015 Mary co-founded Evolve Law, a sales and marketing channel for Traklight, and spoke internationally on change and technology adoption in the legal industry before selling the company to Above the Law. Mary was named to the American Bar Association's Legal Resource Technology Center 2016 Women in Legal Tech list and the FastCase Class of 2016. She also served on the Group Legal Services Association (GLSA) Board and taught both Technology Law and Access to Justice through Technology at Arizona State. Mary is currently on the Executive Committee of the Alternative Dispute Resolution Section of the Washington State Bar Association.

Andrew O'Connor is an investment manager at Augusta Ventures, specialising in developing portfolio funding solutions with a focus on clients in the infrastructure and construction sectors. Prior to joining Augusta, Andrew worked in private practice at Ashurst and at leading Australian domestic firm, Henry Davis York. Andrew holds a Bachelor of Law (Hons) and Bachelor of Economics from the University of New South Wales.

Andy Poole is the legal sector partner at Armstrong Watson, a top 30 UK firm of chartered accountants and financial advisers. Andy heads the firm's nationwide services to the legal sector, covering all of the firm's 17 offices. He has specialised exclusively in the legal sector since 2004 and provides compliance accounting, tax, and SAR services to law firms as well as helping firms to improve by providing benchmarking, strategic consultancy, merger assistance, structural reviews, and training courses. He understands and proactively informs law firms on issues that may impact on them. Andy speaks at national solicitors' conferences and is a regular contributor to the legal press. Andy is co-author of the Law Society's toolkit on financial stability.

Louis Young is co-founder and CEO of Augusta Ventures, the largest litigation funder by case volume. He has broad experience in investment banking, fund management, company start-up, business leadership, and restructuring. Augusta was established in 2013 with offices in the UK, Canada, and Australia with a business model that includes origination, diligence, and monitoring functions to invest in high volumes of cases of any size. Prior to founding Augusta, Louis has held the role of CEO and COO for several investment businesses, among them Normandy Capital Management, Australian Gold Holdings, Colonial Building Company, and Steelview. In addition, he spent 11 years working in Asia and Africa, where he established and successfully sold two drilling businesses. Louis holds an MBA and an LLB from Bond University.

Chapter 1: Good compensation practices during COVID-19

By James D. Cotterman, Altman Weil

We began 2020 in bright spirits and bountiful economic conditions; by early March all that had changed. Now as we approach year-end, we are able to look back at a year like no other in our lifetimes. In March, firms quickly adjusted operations and quite properly began salary reductions to help conserve cash for an uncertain future. Compensation expenses, including partners, generally absorbs 78 percent of fees in law firms, so reducing pay was an absolutely necessary undertaking to conserve cash and sustain a firm. Pay reductions were often tiered by classification and/or overall salary level. The biggest reductions were at the top of the scale and the smallest reductions at the bottom.

In April, many firms applied for and received PPP loans, which were perfectly designed for the law firm business model. These loans provided payroll and rent support to businesses that qualified. As shown above, compensation is a significant expense component. Rent adds an additional six percent of fees to the mix. Law firms had the expertise and remote work capability to navigate the loan application process. As the year unfolded, some firms returned PPP loans as their perceived need diminished, while others were sustained by the support.

As to staffing, leaders knew they needed to retain their core capabilities, even if the team was largely benched for a while. They needed bench strength so they could quickly get back into action when conditions improved. Therefore, the initial goal was to limit furloughs and terminations, at least until more was known about the future. The few terminations and furloughs that did occur early on were largely of individuals who were chronic underperformers pre-COVID and staff members whose jobs disappeared with remote work (such as receptionists and the like).

In our conversations with law firm managing partners this summer and fall, we heard that most felt pretty good overall about where their firms were at that juncture. There was a sense that messaging and actions had been well aligned and effective at holding their firms together. Economic adjustments had worked and, overall, firms were in much better shape than their spring worst-case projections anticipated. Some firms were even close to their original 2020 profit expectations to date – largely due to quick actions to curtail expenditures as COVID-19 got underway in the US.

But managing partners also told us that they remained cautious about the future. How will 2020 conclude and what will 2021 look like? They understood that patience and unity of purpose have limits, and to keep the core team together and engaged into 2021 will require healthy workflow and restoration of pay. Some had already made partial or full restoration to pre-COVID-19 pay levels. Some had even restored pay retroactively. Having done so does not imply that the crisis is over, but that there is better clarity about cash/workflows and how to function remotely even if clarity on the virus remains murky and volatile.

As we entered the traditional post Labor Day end of summer, compensation season began for much of the profession. Law firm leaders, now accustomed to the additional communication efforts necessary to lead a remote workforce and manage morale as the pandemic surged ahead, used September to convene all compensation decision-makers to discuss the unique circumstances of 2020 and map their paths to reach year-end.

The starting point for these conversations was each firm's particular financial position and projections to year-end as well as the messaging that began in the spring and carried through the summer. Key considerations included how to build on previous messaging through to the end of 2020 and into 2021. As to compensation specifically, planning began on how to craft decision policy that supported that messaging, yet reflected the economic and competitive realities at year-end. The importance of this alignment of messaging and decisions was not just for the partners, but for the entire workforce. This cycle, more than any other, has and will benefit from a thoughtful and organization-wide message that carries forward with whatever theme was used at the start of the pandemic.

As we listen to and counsel firm leaders during this unprecedented compensation season, some common themes have emerged:

- "I need to pay the high contributors; the competitive lateral landscape still exists."
- "I don't want to penalize people for shortfalls due to COVID-19."
- "So many of our partners are having years that are atypical of their long-term contributions."

- "We have made select adjustments where the issues have been chronic and existed long before COIVD-19, but they may not be sufficient."
- "Don't let the opportunity of this crisis go to waste – we were forced to change, forced to rethink how we operate, forced to make decisions that were just not previously possible – and it all worked reasonably well."

Leaders understand that their guiding principles for compensation are that pay decisions should:

- Reflect a proportionality to performance – where performance is a combination of various contributions set by both firm and market;
- Consider the risks and efforts undertaken, the learning achieved, and the results obtained to advance the firm's strategic intent;
- Align with the culture and recognize the behaviors necessary to achieve a desired firm work environment (particularly challenging as firms pivoted to and are largely still in a remote work setting); and
- Protect the firm from externally induced departures in a competitive lateral market – which clearly challenges the first guiding principle.

In some firms this year, high contributors may leave some money on the table. That is not a new concept. When I sit with compensation committees during deliberations or debrief them afterwards, the subject of optics and very high contributors pushing money down to others for the collective best interest is frequently part of the dialogue. So, there is precedent in the act of selflessness. But this year, the needs may materially exceed the resources. It may be wise to broach this subject early.

To further complicate this effort, there likely have been a range of responses to this ordeal within each firm. There are individuals who maintained a solid team attitude, who pitched in, who improved their skills, who assisted others, who accepted individual sacrifices for a greater good, and who stepped out of their comfort zone to add value to the firm and its clients. And, not surprisingly, there were those who focused on themselves, protecting their turf (hours, fees and the like). Some reacted out of fear for the great uncertainty embedded in this crisis and may or may not have overcome that fear as the year progressed. Managing partners have commented that these responses – both positive and negative

– left lasting impressions that are now deeply set in their assessments. Adjusting pay decisions based on these views is entirely appropriate. But it should be consistent with ongoing counseling provided throughout the year and part of the feedback provided at year-end.

If 2020 is the year like no other, then its effect on compensation decisions will complicate an already difficult job. But 2020 will likely have lingering influence in a great many firms. Law firms often assess performance across several recent years to avoid volatility in compensation by smoothing out anomalous performance. How to handle averaged performance data is an additional discussion topic in these firms. There might be extreme and opposing scenarios – partners who had a really good year due to the pandemic and those whose year was a disaster. And the volatility, in both individual actuals vs their long-term norms and across the entire firm, is likely to exceed any anticipated level when the smoothing concept was designed. Thus, some firms may temporarily increase the averaging term to dilute the influence of 2020. For example, a three-year average may be increased to a four- or five-year average until 2020 drops out of the mix. Or 2020 may simply be carried with an asterisk appended and handled with subjective due process.

Firms where a partner's share of the profits is set at the start of the year (prospectively managed firms) have already largely locked in participation for 2020. Some of these prospectively managed firms may include a retrospective bonus for some portion of the overall program. The addition of a bonus presents an opportunity to at least partially address 2020 performance volatility. However, these firms must still address the challenges of how to treat 2020 performance when they set 2021 participation, including the longevity of data points discussed in the preceding paragraph.

Firms with heavy formulaic approaches are also locked in. Those firms will have greater certainty in the outcome of their process, but also less leeway to soften the effects of 2020 activity. A great many of these firms will likely be OK with that outcome. It is part of the bargain that they signed on to. However, there may be firms where the formula results just do not feel right to the partners. Those firms may decide to adjust the formula to achieve a result that the partners can support. An adjustment, that does not require subjectivity, is to collar compensation movement – i.e., compensation for 2020 cannot exceed some percentage plus/minus of compensation from prior year(s). Another approach is to create an absolute floor to compensation – providing a safety net. The consequence of providing a floor is that others will be funding that result. Balancing that outcome with the firm's culture will be easier in some firms then others. Best to start early to examine what may be appropriate and to build support for that.

Leaders also understand that law firm compensation is a zero-sum game. There is only so much cash to go around. And the underlying themes of fully paying high contributors while trying to hold others harmless are competing for these limited dollars. Firm leaders should work on extending the consensus built thus far. Part of that work requires candor about where the firm is currently, what year-end projections predict, and what philosophy will guide compensation decision-makers. This year, cultural alignment may be a more significant guiding principle for compensation decisions than at any time in our memory.

Chapter 2: Retaining your pricing confidence in challenging times

By Stuart Dodds, Positive Pricing

Pricing lessons from the previous global financial crisis, little over a decade ago, are still extremely pertinent today for those of us in the legal sector. Although the current cause, magnitude, and environment today differs (sometimes dramatically) we would do well to heed General George S. Patton when he suggested that we "prepare for the unknown by studying how others in the past have coped with the unforeseeable and the unpredictable".

As any good pricing practitioner will tell you given half a chance, the approach to good pricing should not fundamentally change in an economic downturn – the same key principles still apply. For example, the themes of having a differentiated pricing approach (recognizing that not all clients and practice offerings are under pressure), focusing on the value of your offering (after all, the value of your services has not disappeared overnight – often quite the opposite), adapting your pricing approach to your clients' needs, and having robust pricing governance processes in place still remain – albeit with perhaps a few more subtle tweaks today than normal.

Indeed, when preparing to write this chapter I came across some presentation materials I had received during the early global financial crisis. One had been passed down to me from the managing partner of Linklaters at the time (I was still relatively new in my legal pricing role then) and there was also one from the respected pricing consultancy, Simon Kutcher & Partners, who had presented at a pricing conference I had attended. Although prepared by different authors, both had many consistent themes. I would like to highlight two in particular. Firstly, pricing fundamentals are so called for a reason. And the second? Cleaving close to your clients is especially critical at times of economic uncertainty for ongoing success, regardless of your industry or sector. Adopting these steps will certainly help you more easily navigate those potentially tricky pricing conversations you should have had, are – and should be – having regularly with your clients now.

In this chapter, I would like to highlight eight key steps that, once implemented, will ensure a more sustainable and profitable future in the mid- and longer-term for you and your firm, whilst also helping to strengthen your existing client relationships. But before doing so, it is perhaps useful to recognize what has actually changed since early 2020.

When doing so, I do not mean to minimize or diminish the impact recent events have maybe had to some individuals, businesses, or sectors, but when viewed in the wider business of law, I would argue that very little has fundamentally changed. However, what is undeniable is that the pace of change in a number of related areas has rapidly accelerated.

For example, our collective recent experiences have dramatically driven the shift to remote working, meetings, and supporting technologies ("Zoom fatigue", anyone?) and it has similarly put an increased (and much needed) emphasis on many of the core project management principles (especially those around clarity of role, managing expectations, and monitoring). It has once again brought to the forefront the role of client legal operations and legal procurement teams (who were in their infancy in 2008 and 2010) in engaging with their outside counsel providers and seeking "greater value".

It has also perhaps encouraged some law firm clients to look further afield when sourcing their required legal expertise (although as my business partner, Colin Jasper, astutely observed, it also allows larger law firms to offer clients the "greater value" they seek by bringing the best skills to support a matter, irrespective of location and in a cost efficient and effective manner). But should we have already been doing that anyway, changing a potential threat into an opportunity?

And (as Colin also identified) recent events have encouraged an increasing number of law firms to double-down on their internal efforts to productize many of their products and services for their clients, incorporating a broader use of appropriate technologies, resourcing and project management expertise (although this may also bring separate pricing challenges to law firms as we move away from more traditional law firm pricing approaches to a much more iterative pricing strategy, more commonly adopted by fast moving consumer goods).

So, what lessons can we learn from previous economic downturns (taking General Patton's advice on board) and also from what a number of leading law firms have implemented over recent months?

Having spoken with over 80 leading legal pricing directors over the last 12 months as part of a pricing transformation survey we have undertaken, below is a distillation of the top eight themes we have seen emerge time and time again during this period.

Step 1: View pricing as a process

The first, and one that underpins our whole philosophy at Positive Pricing, is the importance of viewing pricing as process. Pricing is not just the fee that we agree with our clients at the outset, but importantly also how we manage the matter and wider client relationship throughout their respective lifetimes from start to finish and ensure we are fairly paid for the work that we do and the value we provide.

Although this sounds daunting – as many people often view law firm pricing as being primarily "event driven", in other words only really engaging on pricing when there is a panel appointment or significant pitch required – it actually provides us with a major opportunity, which leads me onto step two.

Step 2: The power of small changes

When viewing pricing as process, this gives us many more opportunities to proactively influence our pricing and level of client value delivered.

For example, it allows us to think about what the appropriate fee levels are (i.e. the absolute £ or $ number); what the appropriate fee structure should be based on what we feel is most appropriate to the client (e.g. adopting a fixed fee or one where the fee is based on matter outcome and where risk is shared); how we negotiate our fee; how we should best staff the matter; how we should best manage and then when to have our scope or change variation conversations; and when and how we should best approach the client invoice (perhaps the most intimate part of the client relationship – the "was it worth it?" moment).

By making small incremental improvements in one or more of these areas, we have seen law firms being able to realize improved realization of five per cent or more. For a law firm with a revenue of £100m, this can bring £5m of profit immediately to a firm's bottom line. A big number for sure, but if we then consider the number of people having pricing-related conversations with your clients (typically a firm's partners, for sake of illustration let's say ten), the number of conversations held per week (let's say two), the incremental impact or contribution on profit of each decision (let's say £500) and number of weeks of the year this is done (let's say 50), we DO get to a big number very quickly – in this simple illustration, £500,000. But what else can or should we do?

Step 3: Segmenting your clients

Many law firms have implemented client programs and consequently go through some form of client analysis and segmentation, although this can sometimes be quite a static or episodic exercise. If so, now is the time to reflect and review your segmentation approach but this time through both a client and a pricing lens. A significant number of law firms have done just this over the last six to nine months, some even mapping out their client pricing approaches for a period of the next 12-18 months.

Your firm's larger clients, those who are in sectors that at the time of writing have been heavily impacted (such as the airlines, hospitality, or real estate), or other extremely price sensitive clients which the firm may already have, are very likely to seek one or more of (unilaterally) extending existing panel terms; delaying panel decisions for those you have already submitted for; requesting deeper discounts on ongoing/future work; or delaying (or even cancelling) potential matters as they look to prioritize their legal spend. Other clients – who are perhaps not as economically distressed – may also request some of these as they seek to take advantage of ongoing uncertainty.

Conducting this segmentation exercise will enable you to be prepared and have agreed approaches in place prior to the (inevitable) client request. When doing so, segment your client base driven by their likely pricing behaviors (either by client importance and/or sector). This will allow you to proactively identify ways to both help them and mitigate any potential impact to the firm. After all, good pricing, regardless of situation, needs to remain fair for both parties.

But this approach also applies post-pandemic. We have an opportunity to put in place a more structured approach to how we deal with client pricing requests longer-term, identify those clients we should invest in, negotiate with, and perhaps even those we should no longer serve.

Step 4: Helping your clients

A theme you may have already heard but which cannot be stated enough is to focus on the wider client relationship rather than the revenue in times of economic uncertainty. Lessons from the previous downturn highlight that goodwill built will be worthwhile once the current economic environment improves, with the opposite also being true. At this time, it is especially helpful to be proactive and cleave close to your existing clients.

Although not all of your clients may be impacted (or at least vocally stating that they are) that does not mean we should be giving them less attention than our more vocal or demanding ones. Once the dust has cleared from the current pandemic, and once law firm clients take time to reflect how they have been treated by their outside counsel during that time, we want to be on the positive side of the client relationship balance sheet, which means proactively engaging with your clients throughout and identifying ways to support them both individually and on behalf of their firm.

Emphasizing the value and outputs you are delivering to your clients is key so they can clearly see what they are getting and feel they are receiving a tangible return on their current investment. In addition, proactively engaging with them about current ongoing matters and helping them re-evaluate their legal priorities will also stand you in good stead. Helping them to save money now should also help reduce any pressure on your rates later on and also maximizes the likelihood of being paid.

Remember, there are a number of alternative ways to help clients through this (or any) period of uncertainty without needing to resort to discounting that you could and should consider. These include offering deferred payment terms, offering billing credits that can go towards existing bills or future work, or looking at potential changes to matter scope to reduce legal expenditure. For those who feel they need to make a more immediate financial concession for a particular client, as a minimum it is good practice to ensure that any reduced fixed fees, hourly rate reductions, or other forms of client-specific investment are agreed on a time-bound basis, and then reviewed (i.e. in the next three months or for the duration of matter, whichever is shorter).

Step 5: Managing your discounts

In times of economic uncertainty, it is especially important to take a "firm-wide" view of any client investment being made. This puts a much greater emphasis on good pricing governance and oversight and avoids "random" discounting from individual partners (even if this is being done with the best of intentions).

Suggest moving away from hourly rates (and the focus or opportunity this may give to clients to try and drive rates down now and – by extension – in the future) to conducting work using a different fee approach – such as a fixed fee or on a retainer basis where you can apply any appropriate investment irrespective of timekeeper or experience level.

In sum, avoid changing the reference price or rate for specific levels of expertise where you can. Once changed, it can be very difficult to get back to the same level pre-discount. One of the key lessons from a decade ago is that the ratchet of pricing works much easier going down than going up! Some firms who reduced their rates during the global finance crisis took three or more years to get back to parity. Some still haven't.

If you do need to renegotiate existing client rates, resist the temptation to negotiate in numbers ending in fives or zeros due to the adverse impact on firm profit. For many firms, a one percent higher realization typically adds up to three per cent profit. So far, so good. But the converse is also true – with a five percent discount reducing existing profit by up to 15 percent – that can take a long time to recover. Every little bit adds up, as we saw in step two when we looked at the power of small changes.

Finally, remember that poor management of discounts and rates can often have an adverse impact on your brand. Discounting should always be approached with caution and be coordinated within your firm and across similar types of clients and matters. Note that this does not mean that the discounts are the same. Price differentiation should be our friend.

Step 6: Reviewing and refining your practice group pricing approaches

Certain practice areas will be extremely busy during times of economic upheaval – for example, dispute resolution, (currently) COVID-19 related litigation, restructuring, those services related to technology, and also very likely M&A as markets begin to recover.

For those practice areas in demand, you should be charging an appropriate fee for these services, and certainly not discounting unless there is a very good reason to do so (merely being asked to by a client does not count here). Others may have weaker demand (or certain matter types may do) and therefore targeted (and measured) investment for a time-bound period may be required.

But now is also the time to take the opportunity to define and agree practice group-specific pricing strategies, if you have not already done so, for the next six- to 12-month period at least, to encourage greater consistency of approach, messaging, and management of firm investment. Typical themes you may want to address could include how to target the right type of work from the right type of client (and what are their characteristics), how to move the conversation to be more around the value you provide rather than the price, and different approaches to structure different types of matter (e.g. what can be done on a fixed fee, risk sharing, or subscription basis?).

This is relevant for both those practice areas that will flourish during these times and those that will feel more pressure. Encouraging more frequent discussion of pricing themes as part of your firm's practice group meetings can be a simple, but great, start. It also begins to lessen our event-driven view of pricing conversations as we discuss it more frequently and openly.

Step 7: Reviewing and selectively increasing your rates

For many, this theme is the elephant in the room. Firms that do not raise rates during these times will ultimately see a decline in overall profitability as costs will still increase in many areas. In addition, those firms that do not regularly raise rates (even by small amounts) will face much greater obstacles when seeking to recapture any previously forgone rate increases in the future, as their clients get "sticker shock" at the level of subsequent increase being requested.

Take time to review your rates and make an assessment of where and for whom rates may need to change. Even marginal increases (for example, two to three percent) will make a tangible difference to your bottom line. Regardless, these rate increase (as always) should be introduced sensitively and with appropriate consideration to your client(s).

However, in our experience, the rate-setting process is something that many law firms often get wrong – even those with otherwise very strong financial or pricing functions. Rate increases should not be driven by an arbitrary percentage increase, and although market and competitive information is helpful, it should not drive your rate as the value you provide your clients is distinct. Ask yourself who are your busier timekeepers within the firm, who are your clients that are less price sensitive (from our earlier step three) and then honestly assess what the impact of an additional \$10, \$20, or \$50 to your busier timekeepers' rate is likely to make to their overall utilization. Probably very little. Now ask the question as it relates to their profit contribution. Probably a lot.

Step 8: Keeping a clear focus on your cashflow and Accounts Receivable

Our final step is one that many firms are increasingly focusing on – having a continued and improved focus on cashflow and A/R within the firm. This step is important in good times and bad.

A study conducted by Smith & Williamson and summarized in *Legal Week* during the summer of 2019 identified that the Top 50 firms in the UK had £5.6bn of unpaid client invoices. Put another way, this was approximately one-third of this group's total annual revenues still due by their customers at their respective firm's year-end. A staggering proportion. If this is what happens in "good times", with the corresponding impact on a law firm's cash reserves, the impact is bound to be more severe in "bad times" as law firm clients begin to more actively manage their cash flow.

One approach that we have seen taken by some firms is to be more questioning before potentially accepting a new instruction during the pandemic. For example, for all potential new matters (subject to some form of agreed materiality or threshold), determine what the level of recovery is likely to be, what resources will be required, and assess whether this is appropriate for the firm to support given the existing client relationship, client payment profile, and potential fee or profitability. Otherwise, scarce resources may become even scarcer, cash reserves may dwindle, and firm profit may stagnate or even decline.

In closing, adopting one or more of the steps outlined above will go a long way to help you improve parts of your firm's pricing capability and help you come through the current economic turbulence relatively unscathed.

Implementing all eight will help you build and secure a strong pricing foundation for the immediate term and also the times ahead. The approach to good pricing does not fundamentally change in an economic downturn, so make sure to have your solid pricing principles in place.

We opened this chapter with a quotation by General Patton. I would like to end with one too, this time from Henry Kissinger – one that many will have related to over recent months. "There cannot be a crisis next week. My schedule is already full." Just make sure that your schedule includes implementing the pricing fundamentals.

Chapter 3:

Partner performance – becoming and remaining a partner

By Timothy B. Corcoran

Law firms are notorious havens for underperformers. Irrespective of size or location, whether comprised of bright-eyed Ivy grads or night school alums, and spanning all legal disciplines, it's a truism that every law firm has an astounding number of lawyers who simply aren't capable of getting the job done. Or at least it seems that way when lawyers engage in idle chatter about their colleagues' performance.

Law firm cultures can differ greatly, but, to no surprise, there are also commonalities. A consistent theme is that partners – also known as members, shareholders, or principals, depending on the firm's particular business form – are given wide latitude to run their individual practices as they wish, with minimal oversight over the targeting and pursuit of clients, the pricing and staffing decisions necessary to address the client's needs, the service posture adopted by the lawyers delivering legal services, the quality of the legal services rendered, the profitability of the legal services, the client's satisfaction, the methodology to pursue, or not, subsequent engagements from the client, and even key information about the client that might suggest additional opportunities for the firm. Why? Because partners tend to believe that, as owners of the law firm, they can do as they wish.

An undisciplined approach to law firm governance is reminiscent of small children daydreaming about someday being grown, a time that they expect will allow them to do whatever they wish, without constraint, because nobody's going to be the boss of them. This laissez-faire approach to self-governance tends neither to create nor foster the collegiality and harmony that so many law firm websites promote. Indeed, a lack of accountability tends to create tension. *"I wouldn't hire that guy to bury my cat, dead or alive,"* spat one Biglaw partner when this writer praised a recent accomplishment by another of the firm's partners. *"Who's dead or alive, your partner or the cat?"* I asked, amused. *"Doesn't matter, he'd still get it wrong."*

To have under-performance, you must first have performance

We'll return to management and governance anon. First let's point out an inherent flaw in identifying and, ultimately, resolving under-performance. To know when someone is doing their job poorly, you must have a standard of excellence or quality to which their performance can be measured. This self-evident truth is a fundamental assumption in job design, hiring criteria, and performance evaluation systems used in businesses everywhere. It's also critical in other fields. An orchestra relies on an explicit understanding of how to measure the relative capabilities of, say, one trombonist over another. Medical schools, not known for accepting poor students, must have some way to distinguish between exceptional students when selecting candidates for further training in the most advanced disciplines. As memorialized in the 1980s movie "Top Gun," the Navy's flight school instructors were tasked with selecting *"the best of the best"* of naval aviators.

So how do we define exceptional partner performance in a law firm? Opinions vary.

For purposes of hiring new entrants to the firm, a hiring committee, recruiting partner, or practice group leader often establishes the standard. For promotion from associate to partner, some combination of an associate review committee, an associate's mentor, and a vote by all of the firm's current equity stakeholders, whatever their opinions may be, are necessary ingredients. For doling out compensation, most law firms have some combination of objective and subjective criteria, applied in some objective and subjective manner, by a compensation or management committee whose participants and priorities may change from year to year. And lest we forget, clients have the final say in whether a lawyer is worthy of being hired, being paid, being paid in full, and being rehired.

Given the many variabilities, is there any way to establish a common standard? To set the tone, it may be helpful to turn to W. Edwards Deming, the father of the quality movement: *"If you can't describe what you're doing as a process, you don't know what you're doing"*. Those lawyers who insist that quality cannot be quantified perhaps reveal more about themselves than they intend. As the managing partner of a powerhouse litigation boutique shared, *"We don't measure quality. It's impossible to know. We certainly don't believe our clients know. That's why they hire us. We just know it when we see it."* This is the sort of cryptic and elusive statement that's perhaps intended to unironically convey the same message as one of those kitschy "Genius at work" signs adorning office cubicles everywhere. However, to many clients tasked as stewards of their business owners' mission-critical legal supply chain, it sounds a lot like the ravings of an amateur.

The Full Monty

In the absence of an objective standard of quality, law firm leaders default to measures of production. After all, for more than a generation the billable hour has proven to be a useful proxy to measure motivation, endurance, capacity, intellect, marketability, rainmaking prowess, client satisfaction, revenue, profits, and promotability. How simple! Trouble is, the billable hour and its adjacent metrics of utilization, billing realization, and collection realization provide little insight beyond how many hours a lawyer works, how many hours a lawyer bills, and how much revenue a lawyer collects.

Production metrics provide minimal insight into quality, client satisfaction, profitability, attitude, team spirit, or other "intangible" factors that matter so much in any organization. The net result is that partner performance is usually reduced to some combination of billable hours worked, billed, and collected. Little else matters.

Some might ask, what about "origination" or business development? Naturally, the efforts necessary to identify, pursue, negotiate, and win new clients and new matters are critical to the growth of a law firm. But these efforts are substantially ignored. The *result* of these efforts, however, in the form of billable hours worked, billed, and collected matter. They matter a great deal. How one gets there? Not as important.

What about management roles? Mentoring young lawyers? Serving on firm committees? Showing up to all-hands meetings? Showing up to partner meetings, even? How about fiscal hygiene tasks, like entering time, collecting fees, and closing files? Do we value partners who share credit when hunting in packs? Or those who access firm resources in a fiscally responsible way? And, of course, how important is it to act like a grown up licensed professional rather than a petulant toddler? How do all of these factors impact performance metrics? Sadly, these are often lumped into some sort of subjective and intangible "citizenship" category that can be safely ignored so long as other financial contributions are sufficiently notable. When challenged, the recurring and endlessly inexplicable reply from law firm leaders is, "*We know tracking billable hours isn't the best way to measure performance, but at least it's easy to track*".

Nevertheless, production is a necessary element of many lawyers' contributions, and there's nothing wrong with establishing targets. But in a modern legal practice, an undue focus on billing time will create perverse incentives to avoid managing client work more efficiently. So, we must move beyond billable hours and use more advanced metrics such as matter profitability, utilization of firm resources (so that slack capacity is utilized before hiring new lawyers) and client retention and penetration (repeat business and cross-selling). The targets will undoubtedly vary because law firms are multi-line businesses operating in different geographies with different clients that operate in different competitive markets. It makes no business sense to establish equal targets across the board, except for perhaps some rudimentary minimums. In a mature business, performance is typically measured against a pre-defined plan, not compared to unrelated business units with fundamentally different micro- and macroeconomics.

Planning for success

Law firms tend to operate one year at a time. Revenues come in, expenses go out, what's left is divided up amongst the shareholders at year-end, and everything starts anew. This approach, somewhat exaggerated here for effect, places a premium on short-term results and fosters short-term thinking. Compounding this, performance is often measured at only the aggregate level. If the firm did better collectively this year than last year, and shareholders take home more, we can safely ignore any troubling headwinds and avoid tough conversations.

The law firms that do look at individual performance tend to focus on relative results. *"Our average revenue growth is up 4.5 percent,"* the leaders may note, *"And your billable revenue falls close to that range, so well done you!"* However, in a growth market segment, one in which clients are buying and competitors are booking double digit revenue increases, regressing to the mean revenue growth represents significantly sub-par performance. Or in a mature market, marked by client fee pressure, constant threats from law firm and ALSP competitors, achieving even minimal revenue growth might be considered a stellar accomplishment. Ignoring these differences masks underlying market trends that, if proper attention were paid, would likely lead to re-allocations of resources, investment, and compensation.

Law firms with a more business-oriented mindset look at practices and often offices as separate businesses. A remote or newly established office might not enjoy the same brand awareness as a headquarters location, so it needs more visibility. A dominant practice with a long history of deals and accolades might need less general promotion – potential buyers already know the firm – and more emphasis on differentiation. High margin practices that are, at present, immune from client price pressure should focus on client retention and penetration, creating switching costs that insulate the firm from the inevitable reckoning to come. Lower margin practices, facing constant price pressure, should focus on practice re-engineering – investing in process improvement, project management, automation, and innovation – in order to boost margins while maintaining or even improving the quality of services rendered. How do we know where these differences lie? We plan.

For sophisticated businesses, the planning process, while at times tedious, is critical to securing the future. Are we in the right lines of business? Can we generate profits at the prices the market is willing to pay? If not, what can we do differently? What other lines of business should we explore? What unmet needs in the market match up against our specific strengths? How do we best capitalize on this opportunity? Law firms that engage in this recurring process to assess internal and external factors that will impact performance are rarely surprised relative to competitors that blithely march on, unaware of what's looming over the next hill.

There are countless tools, frameworks, artifacts, and levels of rigor that can be used in the planning process. Which to choose and at what level of detail are matters for lively discussion. The only mistake is not selecting and embedding a process at all. Many law firms nod in this direction by asking lawyers to submit an annual individual marketing plan, or ask practice leaders to submit an annual strategy update, or invest every five to seven years in a drawn-out strategic planning exercise that produces a binder full of insights no one will read. So long as billable hours are up, and year over year revenue is growing, the distracting tasks of forward planning are relegated to the "nice to have" category.

The questions posed above, baked into whatever format is simple to compile and simple to act on, will suffice to get started. Law firm leaders should rely on the largely untapped strategic capabilities of their business professionals – busy people, to be sure, but often focused on tactical and nonsensical trivia that fail to improve business performance but comfort partners who equate busy-ness with effectiveness. A culture of planning leads directly to a culture of performance. The ongoing – and not merely year-end – question is: Based on what we know, how well are we doing in *this* market, with *these* clients, with *these* specific resources? What can we be doing differently? Those who exceed expectations earn rewards. Those who fail to meet expectations earn increased scrutiny.

Evaluating performance (AKA where managers earn their pay)

Note that performance is always influenced by the level of rigor put into planning. Some will perpetually under-promise in the hope that over-delivering will earn outsized rewards. Others will eagerly set stretch goals despite well-documented headwinds, and when they fail to meet goals their miss becomes everyone's burden. This is where law firm leaders must exert their managerial muscles. The goal of a good planning exercise is not undue optimism or undue skepticism. It's realism. Every annual plan, and budget, should have a realistic case, a pessimistic case, and an optimistic case. Rewards are pegged to meeting realistic expectations, and performance is measured routinely, on a proactive basis, not in arrears.

As has long been noted, lawyers serving in part-time management roles, regardless of the titles of the offices they hold, tend not to have the training, the time, or the incentives to dig deep into managing. This is a huge, missed opportunity. Some firms are shifting more toward full-time management roles, with a years-long process to identify and groom those who show the aptitude and appetite for management. Others are relying more heavily on C-level business executives, often from outside the legal sector, who are accomplished managers and leaders. Many, alas, would likely invest in management training if they were aware of the accretive benefits of doing so, but due to a career-long indoctrination into the cult of lawyer exceptionalism, it has never occurred to them that they're not already masters of management fundamentals.

Too many firms, however, eschew a more hands-on management style, because law firms are comprised of owners who walk the hallways every day, who strenuously object to being told what to do, and who flex their shareholder clout when challenged. On one occasion, when suggesting to a law firm executive committee a new policy that might begin to curtail several partners' notoriously unprofitable efforts, one of the partners explained to this author, as if indulging a toddler, why this would never happen. *"We don't tell our partners to do anything in this firm. We don't send messages. We don't try to control the partners' actions. We offer advice and best practices. If and how they choose to act is their business, not ours."*

Law firms with a planning culture and strong management do a better job of putting people in a position to succeed. Contributions and therefore expectations will differ by partner, and this calls for more of a "situational management" approach than a one-size-fits-all performance standard.

Carrots and sticks

The path to successful performance is not, as many partners desire, to elect a benevolent leader who will take stock of the enterprise, make the necessary battlefield calls, and dole out compensation fairly. While indeed these benevolent leaders exist – many doing instinctively well what others struggle to accomplish despite significant training – the challenge is that any system heavily reliant on a strong personality is flawed. The same system that allows for a benevolent leader to act unfettered also allows for bad actors, for abuse, and for bias.

In a notable example, a newly elected managing partner visited a small office that had joined the firm two years prior. The office managing partner reported, "*When he came here, it was the first time that most of the lawyers had met him. He held a town hall meeting and announced that the office was significantly under-performing based on some new profitability analysis. But we had just had our two best years due to having access to more lawyers to do the work we brought in, work that we had to turn away before we joined the firm. He said that we needed to do better or he'd be forced to make cuts, and then he left town. My people were in shock. So was I, frankly. I have attended every partner meeting since we arrived but I had never heard of this new profitability analysis, so I had no idea what we could or should be doing differently. I've been practicing law successfully for over 30 years. I've held management roles in two firms. I've never seen such a debacle.*"

Just as critical to performance as the planning process is the evaluation process. Law firm leaders should make accessible all performance metrics that are available, certainly all that will be used at compensation time. These metrics, like the goals established in the individual and practice plans, must be available at the beginning of the year, so there's time to make course corrections when performance falters.

Most firms lament poor systems, or poor data, and for good reason. Nevertheless, if the data can be compiled at year-end for compensation reviews, then it must be compiled regularly during the year.

The goal of the entire performance management system is to manage expectations. Every partner should know what's expected. Every lawyer should have a voice in setting these expectations. Every lawyer should have an opportunity to see how their actions and results are contributing or failing to achieve the desired objectives, so they can adjust. And every lawyer should have a pretty clear sense of the rewards that will ensue if they meet expectations. We can't account, of course, for every eventuality, so partner compensation will always be influenced in part by overall firm performance. In a significantly down year, even those partners who meet expectations might see their rewards dip. In a significantly up year, some partners who have faltered in meeting personal objectives might see a dip in individual compensation partially offset by profit share increases.

We have written at length elsewhere about partner compensation systems[1] but we'll summarize here by saying that a good compensation plan will both *drive* and *reward* desirable behavior. It will delineate the behaviors and performance factors that matter so that partners who embrace the plan will see increasing rewards, and partners who choose not to pursue the necessary behaviors will self-select lower rewards.

All of the planning and evaluation falters, however, if law firm leaders fail to take action. In many of today's law firms, leaders avoid the "tough conversation" because it's uncomfortable. Some avoid confrontation because there's a significant barrier to ousting or de-equitizing a partner, an action that is rarely necessary when management is able to have the tough conversations. Luckily, having a system helps. A planning process to set expectations, the ready availability of performance metrics, and an evaluation process that focuses on actions and outcomes provide a much better context than an awkward conversation about some vague and subjective criteria, which sounds more like an opinionated character attack.

A law firm culture where every partner has the autonomy to make business decisions, good or bad, whether they even know the difference, and then demand increasing rewards poses significant challenges to part-time management. A law firm culture that embraces planning, open communication, where expectations are properly set, that defines and rewards desirable behaviors, and that withholds rewards from partners whose financial contributions are clouded by meaningful gaps in other critical contributions, is one in which partners and management thrive. But to get there requires some effort. Who's ready to get started?

Reference

1 See "The Changing Face of Partnership. Defining and Rewarding the Highest and Best Use," *Human Capital in the New Legal Ecosystem*, ARK Group, 2020, and "Reward Today or Invest in Tomorrow. Aligning Partner Behaviors with the Long-Term Health of the Firm," *Compensation Innovation,* ARK Group 2018, and "Incentivizing the New Normal," *Compensation (Re)Design for Law Firms*, ARK Group, 2016.

Chapter 4:
Pricing, budgeting, and KPIs – all change after 2020?

By Mary Juetten, Traklight

A few years ago, I was asked to write a book about small law firm key performance indicators (KPIs). As I discussed the topic with lawyers and their administrators or accountants, several themes emerged:

- Most lawyers do not understand that they are running a business;
- Most lawyers do not budget or estimate billings or costs for a case;
- Many lawyers do not like numbers yet still try to set pricing for their services; and
- Many firms, of all sizes, set billing rates and compensation based solely on the market.

The year 2020 was tough to say the least but the fundamentals of running a law practice from solo to Big Law remain the same. Understanding the data required to measure performance is important, and learning how to budget, price, and predict revenue is now critical. As we tell our clients, it's fine to seek professional help for technical business aspects such as accounting or technology, but become informed so as to protect your practice, regardless of size.

Law is a business

Without debating the law as a profession versus a business, it's fundamental to assume that any lawyer needs to make a living. Therefore, for solo lawyers or a lawyers in any size firm, understanding the business of legal has an impact on the bottom line. However, a working knowledge of business basics can provide an advantage in the increasingly competitive landscape.

In 2017, Clio's Legal Trends report discussed that slightly less than half of the legal professionals surveyed could estimate their future billings for the upcoming year.[1] Reported in the same year, approximately

60 percent of firms are working without billable hour targets and half of lawyers do not set budgets for matters.[2] In summary, the majority of firms do not seem to have the basic business approach of setting budgets that include revenue targets.

Further, if only 50 percent of lawyers create a budget for a case, that means that clients do not have an idea of their potential legal spend. Personally, having hired an employment lawyer over a decade ago, the idea that my lawyer held a blank check for fees was not comforting during an already stressful period. Although not all client KPIs are financial, lawyers must overcome any aversion to math and finances in order to provide clients with as much certainty and transparency as possible.

Data before decision

One of the frequent questions that I hear concerning performance measurement is "How do I get started with measuring KPIs?", usually followed by "Where do I get the information?".

In their usual legal problem solving mode, many attorneys just want to jump to the best measurement, when unfortunately the answer to getting started with KPIs is within the firm's approach to clients, including processes and data collection.

The saying "garbage in – garbage out" holds for KPIs. In other words, the data has to be timely, relevant, and accurate. The principle of keeping things simple applies to any KPIs and pricing.

Cash is king

Before we dive into KPIs, a word about cash flow. During the early days of the pandemic, I was asked to deliver several talks about budgeting and cash flow. The lessons from those webinars were learned years ago and stand the test of time. There are two ways to improve your bank balance; spend less or make more.

Therefore, preserving your firm's cash includes taking a hard look at expenses with an eye to those costs that can be cancelled, paused, or deferred. Do not be shy about asking because if you do not ask for that reduction or payment plan, it's unlikely that it will just happen. A line-by-line review of all the past year's expenses is a good place to start to see how to both save some money and also prepare your future year's budget.

Unfortunately, one constant is that many law firms have high accounts receivable balances, and often several months' worth of billings remain outstanding. Cash collection is part of most professionals' work; even when I was in finance at a large law firm, I would have lawyers assist with client calls for late account payment. Best practices call for diligent accounts receivable management – but by upfront billing, using retainers where permitted (including automatic replenishment of those amounts), and setting realistic collection policies, lawyers can ensure solid cash flow. If an account is late, ensure you talk with the client and create a workable payment plan.

My approach is always to think of billing as only part of the final step, a matter not complete until the cash is in your bank account. And to take it a step further, truly not finished until you evaluate your client's level of satisfaction.

KPI basics

As discussed, cash is the life blood of any business and, therefore, law firms of all sizes. It follows that any KPI system should have the client – your source of cash – as a top priority for measurement. Client satisfaction is a critical KPI and the net promoter score (NPS) is now widely known in the law and recommended for obtaining customer feedback in all industries. However, KPIs should be based on the flow of work or processes within a firm to ensure that they are tailored to how legal services are provided to clients.

The following framework with seven areas of measurement[3] is useful for planning KPIs for your firm. Please note that these are laid out in the order of how a matter comes up and is dealt with, billed, and closed within a firm, and not in any order of importance.

- Client development;
- Client acquisition cost (CAC);
- Productivity;
- Profitability;
- Performance;
- Client experience; and
- Firm culture.

I would also add compensation as an area to explore as well as pricing but both those topics use the data from the KPIs to inform their calculations. Each of these areas have processes that should be understood before deciding how to measure success. Also, it's important to not try and implement too many KPIs all at once.

In a second book, I built upon the idea of obtaining data before decision-making and outlined the need to review firm goals and processes before any purchase of technology.[4] In addition, I explored how to evaluate pain points in a practice to know when and what data to gather to review and adjust processes and develop appropriate KPIs.

Five common KPIs

As mentioned above, it's crucial to understand your firm or practice goals and high-level areas for improvement, before embarking on a measurement exercise. For example, if you have a cash challenge and your accounts receivable are all paid up to date, then you must check profitability on the largest matters and, in turn, your pricing.

To illustrate, here are five KPIs that are commonly used by many when they are experiencing challenges (or pain) as follows:

Challenge	Framework	KPI
1. Not enough client work	Client development	Client prospect pipeline
2. Cash shortage	Profitability	Aging tolerance
3. Busy but miss targets	Performance	Billings collected
4. Tight matter margins	Profitability	Contribution margin
5. Unhappy clients	Client experience	Net Promoter Score

Some of the below are borrowed from outside the law and the terms may not be familiar, but these are business concepts that will help your practice. Understanding these basics will help with the links between KPIs, budgets, and pricing.

KPI #1 – Client prospect pipeline

The idea of a pipeline comes from the sales industry. A list is made of potential customers with a value of the upcoming work and estimates of how likely that project and sale is to happen, usually at 25 percent, 50 percent, 75 percent, or 100 percent. The example below is where the project is a go at 100 percent, or in other words, the client is going to hire someone (the "Go") but is evaluating two law firms. You feel your chances are equal so you can say 50 percent for the "Get" or success percentage.

Client – $15,000 potential revenue.
100% Go
50% Get
$7,500 value in the pipeline ($15,000 x 100% x 50%)

You would go through your prospects methodically to calculate all the potential sales in your pipeline and then adjust for the Go and Get percentage by multiplying. Small firms use a simple excel sheet but some client relationship management (CRM) systems include this information so that your pipeline is kept up to date as you input data on your business development efforts.

However, like budgets, these are estimates and should not take hours to develop. The total value in the pipeline would be compared to the amount of business that you need to generate to stay profitable. If you find that your pipeline is low, then you may need to consider increasing your marketing efforts.

KPI #2 – Aging tolerance

Lawyers are human and most of us do not like to ask for money, even when we have delivered our services. I have chatted with many lawyers who focus on billing but not collection. If I ask how long it takes on average to collect their receivables or how much is outstanding, many do not know. Until billings (whether hours, flat fee, or contingency) are collected from clients, there is no point measuring how much was on the invoices.

A simple metric is the aging tolerance, which is the amount of accounts receivable that you can tolerate being late, defined by a set number of days – usually 30 or 60. You then look at your total invoiced for the month and see how much of your outstanding accounts receivable are over the threshold days. Most accounting or practice management systems include an aged accounts receivable listing that can be run monthly for this KPI.

Accounts receivable greater than 60 days	$104,688
Total firm billings for the month	$495,000
Aging tolerance KPI	21%
Target aging tolerance KPI	10%[5]

The example above shows that this firm established a target that no more than ten percent of its monthly billings would be outstanding for longer than 60 days. This target means that they should be collecting 90 percent of all the billings within the 60 days, otherwise they may have cash flow issues. As the numbers show, the calculated aging tolerance is more than double, meaning that a cash flow problem may be looming. The next step would be to review the aged accounts receivable list and take action to collect these bills.

KPI #3 – Billings collected

Further to the idea of cash collections, measuring an attorney's success based on billings alone does not align the individual and firm goals. A lawyer will bill as much as they can unless they are held to a budget and measured against what is ultimately collected for their effort, sometimes referred to as realization.

Traditional utilization looks like the following:

Billable hours target	1,800
Hours billed	1,950
Utilization	108%

At first glance, this busy attorney is doing well but it's an incomplete view if the matters are over-budget or the cash is never collected. The KPI that takes all this into account is as follows:

Budgeted revenue	$360,000 (1,800 hours at $200 per hour)
Billings collected	$350,000 (after write-offs/uncollected amounts for 1,950 hours)
Billings collected KPI	97%

This KPI also supports the "cash is king" concept, plus the lawyer's compensation should be tied to overall collections, as long as the lawyer is aware of the budgets, targets, and individual performance goals. Aligning firm culture and goals with individuals' targets and compensation is fundamental to success, and should be part of all firms' planning.

KPI #4 – Contribution margin

This concept comes from accounting and involves treating clients as mini-profit centers by grouping the revenue and expenses from similar matters in order to analyze the amount left over for contribution to firm general and overhead expenses. In other words, you break down the overall revenue and expenses into categories.

Using an excerpt from a family law firm contribution example,[6] the contribution in dollars and then in percentage can be compared across matters. Establishing the grouping of matters and the average client fees would come from an analysis of the most recent year's results adjusted for any outliers or situations that are unlikely to repeat. This type of analysis is not precise and having an accountant help with these estimates may make sense for those not comfortable with finances.

To illustrate how the information in the chart below can be used:

- *Separation – no kids* matter yields a $1,000 contribution from a $2,000 fee but the *Complex separation* yields only $2,000 from an $8,000 fee. So if the *Complex* does take four times as much of your time, you are not getting four times as much contribution.
- The same holds true for the *Divorce* categories.
- This information is important if you have to choose between clients but even then you can decide to staff differently depending on the contribution.

FFL contribution chart	Average client fees	Contribution (amount left over after matter costs)	Contribution as a % of fee	Notes
Separation – no kids	$2,000	$1,000	50%	Basic agreement to separate and filing
Separation – basic with kids	$4,000	$1,800	45%	
Complex separation – kids / company	$8,000	$2,000	**25%**	
Divorce – basic no kids	$10,000	$6,000	60%	For more complex cases, expert witnesses are billed separately at cost and are removed from the calculation
Divorce – basic with kids	$20,000	$8,000	**40%**	
Complex divorce with kids / company	$80,000	$16,000	**20%**	
Enforcement – child support, custody, alimony and modification	$4,000	$2,000	50%	Includes court representation if necessary
Consultation; child support; modification; paternity; name change	$2,000	$1,300	65%	Miscellaneous matters that include filing but not court appearance
Adoption	$30,000	$3,000	**10%**	Only two adoptions per year over past three years

By reviewing the contribution margins above, the ones in bold are those that need more investigation as to why the results are comparatively low. Is it the staffing, the approach, or the fees? Note that this contribution margin KPI can be used also to evaluate flat fees and the billing rates used for the matter.

KPI #5 – Net Promoter Score (NPS)

The NPS KPI is from outside the law but has gained popularity over the past five years. In a nutshell, clients answer the following questions:

> *On a scale of 1 to 10, how likely are you to recommend <insert name of firm> to <others (friends, family, clients, businesses)>? (1 is extremely unlikely and 10 is extremely likely). Why or why not?*

For the first question, numeric responses are categorized as follows:

- 1 to 6 – Detractor
- 7 or 8 – Neutral
- 9 or 10 – Promoter

The number of responses are tabulated and then the NPS is calculated by subtracting the detractors from the promoters, leaving the neutrals out of the formula. By way of a quick example, if there were 55 responses (38 promoters, ten detractors and seven neutrals), the scoring would yield an NPS of 51 percent.[7]

This calculation can arrive at a score that ranges from -100 percent to 100 percent; the negatives happen if there are more detractors than promoters. That said, a single NPS score by itself is not meaningful, rather it's important to benchmark with others within the legal industry and also over time within your own firm.

The second question builds on being client-centric. It's important to ask for the reasoning behind their response. In my experience, valuable information about you and your team's performance is gathered with this single question. Finally, do not use anonymous NPS requests because you cannot follow up with the client when needed.

The "I" in KPI

As you saw above, the continuum starts and ends with clients. I cannot stress enough the requirement to be client-centric or meet your client where they are in the metaphorical sense, not necessarily in person.

Again, you must tailor the choice of KPIs to your practice's pain points. The measurement is not for the sake of ticking a box to be done with the monthly KPIs. Also, a reminder to go back to the idea of garbage in – garbage out; ensure your data collection is sound.

KPI measurement is done to provide "indicators" or indication of various aspects of firm performance but there should be targets that stem from predictions and budgets. These KPIs provide information for pricing, plus there is a link between costs, budgets, and KPIs.

Budgeting is an art, not science

Zero-based budgeting is a concept that translates into a simple re-building from the ground up of expenses and revenues each year. In other words, instead of rolling over last year's firm billings and adding or subtracting a percentage, you build up your budgeted revenue based on actual predictions by type of case. Also, you need to budget monthly revenue targets based on history adjusted for current realities of demand or your availability, rather than dividing the total budgeted annual billings amount by 12 months to have the same target each month.

A similar approach holds for expenses but the budget is an opportunity to do an annual review of what is needed to run the firm on a line-by-line approach. Think of expenses as two types – direct, to provide services to your clients, and general firm overhead costs. The latter is where there can be savings by reviewing whether all subscriptions and commitments are necessary.

When it comes to revenue, that is where pricing deserves a deeper dive.

Pricing requires old math

Over 15 years ago, in what seems like a lifetime after 2020, I was the director of finance at one of Canada's largest law firms. I was brought in during a merger of three firms and gravitated towards the business lawyers and specifically the litigation practice. Most of the partners would give a WAG (wild ass guess) for the budget on their cases and, back then, clients accepted that approach for fee estimates. The world was still either billable hours or on a contingency basis, with maverick lawyers using flat fees as the rare exception. Unfortunately, that appears to still be the norm.

Recently, I was looking to hire a law firm outside of the US and they proposed both a retainer plus contingency fees for a claim resolution. To me that seems to be a misunderstanding of the connection between value and pricing.

The two angles to view pricing are from the client and the attorney perspectives. For the client, they look for certainty or as much predictability as possible with a low risk of wasting their money. Also, the client's willingness to pay a billable or flat rate is an indication of market value.

For the lawyer, the math kicks in as the amount to be charged needs to cover your direct costs and yield enough to contribute to overhead and profit regardless of the type of billing.

Hourly rate

Using a solo lawyer as an example of an hourly rate calculation, the first step is to make estimates of the following:

Take-home pay	$100,000
Matter expenses	$4,000
Overhead	$46,000
	$150,000[8]

If this lawyer works 1,000 hours that he could bill and collect to generate $150,000 to pay all the bills and pay himself, the hourly rate would be $150 ($150,000 divided by 1,000 hours). If this lawyer can command that amount from his clients, then both sides of the calculation work.

Flat fees

As we move to flat or fixed fees, the theory is similar but now the calculation focuses on the contribution for the various types of matters (see KPI #4 above). That contribution margin must cover both the firm's overhead and the profit (or take-home pay). Let's assume in our example that with the overhead at 30 percent and profit at 15 percent, the minimum contribution margin is 45 percent. However, please note that the larger dollar cases will impact the overall average more, so if these are less than the 45 percent, there have to be others that contribute more in terms of percentage.

Using the same numbers as above from the example, new flat fees are set to improve the contribution margin. Similar to billable hour rates, these flat fees should be tested with the relevant market, plus any feedback from past clients can also inform these changes.

FFL pricing chart	Average client fees	Contribution as a % of fee	New flat fees	New contribution as % of fee
Separation – no kids	$2,000	50%	**$2,500**	**60%**
Separation – basic with kids	$4,000	45%	**$5,000**	**56%**
Complex separation – kids / company	$8,000	25%	**$12,000**	**50%**

The above is similar for contingency fees if you treat each type of case as a small, medium, or large and take some past data to create average contribution.

In summary, it's always important to think of clients first because that is where the cash and profit come from, regardless of the world economic situation. Also remember that the data and the math should inform your decisions, but it's not a science – there are assumptions and qualitative input to consider. Finally, if KPIs and math are not in your wheelhouse, it's perfectly acceptable to outsource this analysis to a financial professional.

References

1 Clio Legal Trends Report, available at www.clio.com/resources/legal-trends/2017-report/.
2 Id.
3 *Small Law Firm KPIs: How to Measure your Way to Greater Profits*, Mary Juetten, Thomson Reuters (2016) p.18.
4 *The Business of Legal: The Data-Driven Law Practice*, Mary Juetten (2018).
5 *Small Law Firm KPIs: How to Measure your Way to Greater Profits*, p.96.
6 *The Business of Legal: The Data-Driven Law Practice*, p.43.
7 38 promoters minus ten detractors is 28 net promoters and divided by the 55 responses is 50.9%.
8 *The Business of Legal: The Data-Driven Law Practice*, p.61.

Chapter 5: The impact of COVID-19 on legal service delivery and client expectations

By Richard Brzakala

Prior to COVID-19, ask any law firm managing partner or CFO to honestly tell you what their firm's primary existential priorities were and they would probably say, "Increasing profitability and market share, investing in the right people and technology, and maintaining and attracting new clients". Things like technological innovation, business optimization, process transformation, information security, relationship management, and service delivery effectiveness have also been important, but for many firms these initiatives have traditionally been secondary, strategic components that took a back seat to maintaining profitability in the face of hyper-competitiveness. COVID-19 not only has acerbated an already hyper-competitive legal marketplace, but it has changed the dynamics of legal competitiveness and perhaps forever changed the delivery of legal services model by moving all of those "back seat" strategies into the "driver's seat" as the world has become increasingly more virtual and digitized.

As we move past COVID-19 and into the new legal marketplace, law firms are on the cusp of having to make an important decision as they prepare to resume business: Do we go back to *business as usual* or embrace all of the *advancements and efficiencies* brought on by COVID-19? It is a pivotal moment for many firms and important enough to shape their destiny and impact their profitability. The answer is easy and evidenced all around us as many businesses in all types of industries have transformed themselves, adapted to change, innovated, and advanced their business transformation at lightning speed, all in order to service their clients who – as they did prior to COVID-19 – continue to demand change and influence service delivery.

The new legal marketplace

In the new legal marketplace (transformed by COVID-19), adopting change and innovation is no longer just an option for a firm, it is an absolute necessity for those firms that want to maintain profitability and competitiveness. Quite simply, it is no longer just about the law, but just as importantly about the business, value, and delivery of the law.

Never in the history of the modern legal marketplace has there been a clearer and more definitive moment to accept change. For many firms looking to develop strategies for a post-COVID-19 world, going back to resume business operations must include a whole new paradigm of thought, strategic thinking, and a recognition that clinging to the status quo (i.e. the past) in terms of business procedures is not enough and that a resumption of business should not minimize the importance of how business operations and service delivery has changed due to COVID-10.

I was shocked when a CFO told me a few months ago that "I can't wait for this COVID thing to end and everything to go back to normal and the way things were". His comment was made not in the context of how devastating COVID-19 has been on society's health and mental well-being, but more so out of an urgency to resume old business practices prior to COVID-19. I thought his comment hardly an endorsement for change and moving forward. It got me thinking about how many more professionals were out there secretly hoping for a resumption of business practices based on the "good old days" – ironically only 12 months ago.

Buying legal services

Regardless of which side of the fence a firm is on, the market continues to be driven by the buyers of legal services – those corporate clients who will demand more for less, more expeditiously and efficiently. Market forces driven by these clients will demand change from their legal service providers and compel them to embrace the new processes we have all grown accustomed to since COVID-19 began.

COVID-19 has transformed the legal marketplace and forced many firms to pivot to new internal business processes such as work from home arrangements that have taken center stage, coupled with virtual communications and increased utilization of digitization tools. Like it or not, transitioning to new business procedures has become for many legal service providers an absolute necessity in order to grow or maintain market share and client loyalty. Those firms that have not been able to make the transition to the new legal marketplace and meet the expectations or service levels demanded by their clients risk being underutilized and uncompetitive.

COVID-19 has not only been a game changer in terms of automation and digitization, but it has also offered law firms a rare opportunity to recognize the need to leap into the second millennium and embrace change far beyond previously thought strategies. Resumption of business should not include resuming old practices and assuming things will return to normal. I have heard many in the media refer to the post COVID-19 period as the "new normal". I disagree with that statement as the new marketplace is far from any normalcy. Normal no longer exists as it has been transformed and replaced by a new service model with a greater responsibility on service providers to deliver excellent service more expeditiously and efficiently.

Client expectations beyond COVID-19 will mean that firms will need to be more open to adapting to change and less reticent or apathetic to adopting new technology. Clients will increasingly be attracted to legal service providers – not necessarily traditional law firms – that are innovative and progressive in their strategies and those providers that are willing to embrace digitization, collaboration, business optimization, and strategic thinking that can enhance the client experience and deliver services to the client more efficiently and cost effectively than before. Please note that I intentionally omitted excellent legal advice as that is an automatic assumption and prerequisite for any and every firm or service provider.

The COVID-19 transformation

COVID-19 has not only transformed how we utilize technology but it has impacted the relationship dynamic between client and law firm. Service delivery and the relationship dynamic that previously existed between a client and its law firm has been changed in multiple ways because of the pandemic.

A good example of the ubiquity of change is how communication and connectivity have universally (it seems almost overnight) grown between firms and their clients by leveraging technology tools that allow for virtual video conferencing, collaboration, and instant messaging. As social distancing and containment lockdowns took hold in many communities these communication tools replaced close contact and in-person meetings and have become invaluable to maintain business operations.

Even as vaccinations start to take hold, there is a general expectation that virtual meetings will become more of the steady state as both clients and firms rotate employees in and out of what will remain of traditional office space in the post-COVID-19 period. A friend of mine commented last summer that she has never in her ten-year legal career felt more connected to her clients than during the pandemic. Although virtual meetings can never replace the social dynamics and intimacy of physical interaction, the productivity gains, efficiencies and effectiveness, and ease by which many clients have been able to connect to their law firms, saving time, resources, and cost, has not been lost on many in-house GCs looking for opportunities to create efficiencies with their staff and lasting cost savings with lower infrastructure costs.

Prior to COVID-19, in-person meetings (i.e. face time) were crucial in helping a firm win work or to help negotiate a deal. Moving forward, firms will need to become increasingly more innovative in how they establish contact, update, negotiate, follow up, market, and ultimately compete for legal work.

Just because COVID-19 arrived does not mean that the legal marketplace became less competitive. I believe that the competitiveness that existed prior to the pandemic has only intensified. Moreover, as much as COVID-19 has been a positive catalyst for technological change, it may also have set the table for possibly destabilizing the transactional relationships some firms enjoy with their clients, as COVID-19 has helped usher in a never-before-seen global labor arbitrage, changing the competitiveness of the legal landscape.

Where once before we saw the advent of alternative legal service providers (ALS), we now see greater opportunities for all types of para-professional service providers (PPSPs) in a virtual world where legal resources no longer have to be in close proximity to a client's market but can be found anywhere and at any price. This has become increasingly true for legal work that is highly transactional, administrative, or commoditized, and can be delivered more efficiently and expediently using technology and artificial intelligence tools. Firms should be prepared for the challenge that PPSPs bring to the new legal marketplace. Market competition for new transactional work will be fought virtually, not in person, against PPSPs that are less structured, nimbler, and technologically secure, and – above all else – laser-focused on winning the legal work at all cost.

As much as PPSPs present a challenge, they also bring opportunities for firms to revisit their service models, optimize resources and technology to demonstrate their competitiveness and cost-saving abilities to existing clients. Legal operations specialists have inherited much of the responsibility, both in-house and at firms, in leading the charge for either helping a firm win more work or developing closer ties to existing clients. In the case of in-house legal teams, legal ops professionals, not lawyers, have grown in greater importance and value to GCs as companies transition into the new legal marketplace and increase their focus on cost containment, compliance, and risk management strategies.

I believe that with the transformation of legal service delivery there has also come a need for firms to reevaluate their strategic vision to better understand how to remain competitive in a post-COVID-19 world. In the face of increased competition, firms lucky enough to enjoy preferred counsel status on a client's panel should double down and invest their energy and resources in doing everything they can to maintain and grow existing historical client relationships. It's a lot easier and more cost effective to maintain an existing client than it is to risk resources and capital in trying to win a new client.

Clients who have existing formalized relationships with firms don't typically want to upset the composition of their panels unless absolutely necessary. This has and continues to be a trend moving into the post-COVID-19 period where clients are looking to retain legal partners who are invested in their relationship, understand their business models and risk strategies, and share the client's cultural and ethical views.

Pricing approaches

However, as economic pressures continue to intensify for both the buyers and sellers of legal services, the cost for legal services will certainly impact the relationship dynamic between clients who are becoming increasingly fiscal prudent versus firms that are struggling to make up lost revenues and improve profit margins. For much of 2020, market capitalization has varied across many industries with some more impacted by COVID-19 than others. Initially with the arrival of COVID-19, many regions and business sectors experienced a decline and a pull back for legal services, especially in highly transactional or commoditized areas. Firms smart enough to understand the economic climate backed away from approaching their clients for price increases. But now as we enter 2021 and markets are slowly recapturing ground, there may be greater leniency in the legal marketplace for firms to revisit their pricing arrangements.

Regardless of the approach a firm takes on pricing its work, there will be a multitude of internal economic and empirical factors, such as cost of labor, underlying technology, overhead, expertise, complexity, practice area etc. to consider as part of a pricing strategy. Then there are the external client factors such as type of client, relationship, volume of work, budget constraints etc. Perhaps the most important and *subjective* consideration to weigh is the impact of any increase on the overall relationship the firm has with its client.

The biggest mistake that I have seen in all of my years of legal operations consulting has been where firms implement a ubiquitous approach – across the board pricing – for all their clients. Firms tend to forget the cardinal rule; that not every client is alike and certainly does not want to be treated that way. In the new legal marketplace, there will be greater focus on moving away from the hourly rate model and more focus on whether or not the firm delivered value in its services. Clients will expect firms to adopt many of the business optimization practices that they have implemented within their corporate structures to look for ways to become more cost efficient and create cost savings. Clients will expect firms to become more introspective with regards to controlling overhead and costs rather than simply rely on the hourly rate model for their profitability. Therefore, coming out of the pandemic, firms should tread lightly and cautiously with their clients around how or when to approach the topic of rate increases.

Correlated to the pricing dynamic and challenge of maintaining profitability are also the non-quantifiable value indicators that impact the relationship between a client and its firm. Value indicators are critical components to any relationship dynamic. Things like excellent communication, understanding the client's business needs and service level expectations, risk appetite, chemistry, trust, reliability, and cost transparency are extremely important in helping a firm maintain client loyalty, distinguish itself from its competition, and grow a firm's revenue stream with a client. In other words, sustaining and maintaining a relationship (i.e. status quo) may supersede a tactical need to play "catch up" with regards to rate increases.

The business of law in the new legal marketplace will require that a firm incorporate value indicators into its business strategy. As much as COVID-19 has moved us all away from the physical to the virtual and increasingly digitized world, what has not changed are clients' expectations around delivering value indicators.

Client expectations

Legal service delivery, going forward, will require that firms treat every client uniquely, understanding and being committed to their client's expectations and requirements. Clients will be increasingly attracted to firms and service providers that have adopted value indicators into their client servicing strategy and that can proactively demonstrate that they live by that strategy. Simple actions such as having a dedicated client relationship manager, frequent communication and updates, and leveraging all tech and social media tools to stay connected speak volumes with many clients who are quick to recognize deficiencies with some firms as nothing more than superficial commitments disguised in nicely crafted marketing slogans.

As mentioned earlier, despite the many positive changes that have taken place in the legal landscape, client expectations have not changed because of COVID-19. Many clients continue to have the same (high) expectations from their firms moving forward as they did prior to the pandemic. Quality, performance, timeliness, and professionalism continue to be critical components in how clients measure the value they receive from their firms. I believe that the challenge for many firms moving into the new legal marketplace will be to not only continue to deliver on client expectations, but also how it can strategically position itself and distinguish itself from its peers.

Not only must firms be prepared to focus their energies and resources on becoming more client-centric, collaborative, tech-enabled, diverse, and agile, but they must also consider their strategic positioning in relation to internal capabilities versus market demand.

For years, some larger firms have been chasing large institutional clients by trying to promote an "all or full service" capability with expertise in a multitude of practice areas to service all of a client's legal needs. While conceptually impressive, this strategy has been less than successful as large corporate clients seldom put all of their eggs into one basket and typically distribute their legal work across various firms and a multitude of legal experts.

Choosing to focus on a specific, strategic practice area(s) and developing a service model specializing in one or a few specific groups of practice areas, as opposed to a full-service model, will not only distinguish a firm from its competitors, but may be a more sustainable business strategy that delivers better results in the long run.

Strategic change

One of the biggest lessons from COVID-19 for firms (and clients) has been the ability to pivot, to be agile, and prepared to implement change. Someone once said that the essence of strategy is not just knowing what you want to do, but also what you don't want to do. Clients will demand excellent service going forward that will probably never change. Focusing on clients' needs, understanding their requirements or even their business strategy is important to sustain long-term relationships. But firms should be very careful not to confuse client focus with the ability to service all types of clients in all areas of the law. That could be disastrous as we move into a post COVID-19 era where clients are looking for leaner, smarter, and more efficient service providers.

In the new legal marketplace, clients will care less about whether a firm has 800 professionals on staff or eight, or whether the firm's offices are located on Wall Street or Main Street. They will be more focused on hiring the best legal professional or a small group of professionals at a reasonable cost to solve a legal issue and deliver on their expectations. Trying to be all things to all clients taxes a firm's resources, time, and money, and risks undermining the quality of work a firm can provide to all clients, all the time.

Not only should firms revisit their internal composition and practice areas from a strategic perspective, but as we move into the new legal marketplace, firms also should look introspectively and holistically at their operations. A firm's success going forward is not just measured by a handful of legal experts (i.e. rainmakers) that haul in the big deals. Sure, in some cases rainmakers contribute significantly to generating revenue, but to be consistently successful (with all clients), maintain client loyalty, and grow competitive advantage, success (and ultimately profitability) is measured by all of the activities and all of the resources a firm has to contribute and not just one or two parts.

Competitive advantage for a firm will also be challenged on the field of diversity and inclusion (D&I), which once again grabbed global attention in the summer of 2020 and reminded all of us just how much more work we all have to do with respect to recognizing, respecting, and accepting human diversity as a principal tenet in our personal as well as business lives. To that end, regardless of a firm's composition, size, or clientele, the most valuable resource at a firm is its people. Every employee at a firm counts, not just the lawyers. Every interaction with a client is crucial for a firm. Every interaction presents an opportunity to either entrench or lose a client. Like infosec, D&I will increasingly become standard for many corporate clients looking to partner with progressive and innovative legal service providers. Firms must be prepared to back up their D&I with actions as clients will be increasingly looking for ways to monitor and measure their service providers' commitment and progress on D&I principles and values.

Marketplace competition will continue to present challenges to many firms, as will client demand and their expectations. Distinguishing oneself in the post-COVID-19 marketplace will also require that a firm increase its investment in technology solutions and information security that help them become more trustworthy and reliable in the eyes of a client. Nothing is more valuable to a client than its confidential information and clients are becoming increasingly focused on information security as table stakes that can make or break a relationship.

Transforming legal service delivery

Going forward, every firm will have to weigh the value of its cost expenditures versus the return on its investment as it moves into the new legal marketplace. Good profitable firms understand the importance, and difference, between what should never change and what should be open to change. It speaks to a firm's ability to manage continuity and change. As much as COVID-19 has transformed legal service delivery, not all firms require a revamping of everything that has been sacred to them. Some firms may be further along in their technological and relationship evolution with their clients than others, so the cost or investment in having to change may be less painful than for others.

Firms should size up their clients and understand the investment they need to make in order to comply with any changes a client requires. Corporate in-house departments are becoming increasingly reliant are looking to goals such as controlling legal costs, improving business optimization, information security, and digitization opportunities around service delivery – not just with their firms, but also their client base. In order for firms to grow revenue, and maintain competitiveness or client loyalty, they must understand how to help clients achieve their goals and whether or not it is worth a firm's effort to pursue certain clients. Not all clients are alike and hold the same promise of profitability.

Lastly, the legal marketplace will continue its evolution (post-COVID-19) as clients will continue to move the pendulum on requiring their service providers to be more innovative and agile and provide value through their processes and work product. The challenge and the question firms should be asking themselves is how prepared they are to embrace that change and are they willing to move forward, carve out opportunities, and distinguish themselves from their market peers.

Where there is challenge, there is opportunity. Buyers of legal services will be attracted to those service providers that can demonstrate a commitment to change, move beyond structural traditionalist views, embrace innovative thinking, and provide an assurance that they respect all of their employees and can deliver excellent legal work, service, and security. In the new legal marketplace, there will be very little accommodation for reticence or apathy when it comes to accepting the new legal service delivery model. Progress and profitability will belong to those firms that can accommodate and move forward beyond COVID-19 and not backwards.

Chapter 6:
Options for law firm financing in difficult times

By Andrew O'Connor and Louis Young, Augusta Ventures

The five typical financing options available to law firms

Even when operating in business-as-usual conditions, the typical "thin reserves" business model adopted by many law firms leaves little head-room for the unexpected. When faced with a major stress event such as the impact of COVID-19, the legal services industry found itself particularly exposed. With clients seeking to preserve their own cash by delaying payments, or deferring projects, income for many law firms will be down. With significant fixed costs of well-paid staff and expensive prime location rents, there is considerable overhead that cannot easily be reduced. As many firms are thinly capitalized, the need for suitable sources of finance that have short-term benefit but do not constrain the firm in the long-term has never been greater.

Of the myriad finance options available, five are likely to be under active consideration by law firm leaders – working capital optimization; bank overdraft facilities; internal funds (partner calls); government Coronavirus support; and litigation finance for cases or portfolios. Each has benefits and costs, and some of these levers will be more familiar to management teams than others.

Working capital

Managing Lock-Up is familiar to many law firm partners. Timely issu-ance of bills and chasing payments are established disciplines. The challenge today is that clients, who themselves are under liquidity pres-sures, are pushing back on paying bills already issued. On top of this, partners may also be reluctant to chase unpaid bills, let alone issue new ones, to avoid damaging relationships. Some firms may look to use a factoring company to provide immediate cash flow, but this may suggest the firm is distressed. Others may seek to delay payments to their own suppliers, but this risks reputational damage. A balance must be found to secure cash today without causing longer-term damage.

Bank overdrafts

Firms will have established credit facilities with one or more lenders. Where good relationships exist, and covenants allow, it may be possible to seek an extension of agreed facilities in the short-term. Whilst base rates have fallen, banks will apply risk-based pricing to any new facilities granted, which may mean costs are prohibitive. Firms will also need to consider the long-term impact of liabilities taken onto their balance sheets – debts will one day need to be repaid and such repayment will generally be guaranteed by the partnership. For many firms, bank facilities will be low down the list of preference but may be the default choice where limited knowledge of alternatives exists.

Partner finance

Often seen as a last resort, seeking funding from partners remains an option for many. For some firms, this may be in the form of delaying or reducing partner distributions. This will probably be unpalatable but is usually speedy to implement. Other firms may look to tap partners to inject further equity. This is likely to be particularly difficult in current circumstances due to the personal impact it will have on colleagues in both the short- and long-term. Partner finance is politically unpopular but is likely to be on the agenda of many management teams who have not yet explored other options.

Government support

In many jurisdictions this is a rapidly evolving area with numerous options, the benefits and costs of which are yet to become clear. Facilities coming on stream include grants for furloughed and sick staff wages, deferred VAT bills, loans for small and medium-sized enterprises and debt facilities for larger business backed by government treasuries and central banks (though in practice the collateral for these lines of credit may not vary from the bank's required pre-scheme). Managers should explore all options but be aware that these facilities are unlikely to be long-lasting, nor cover the full extent of lost income. There is also likely to be pressure at some point to repay these facilities, particularly if it is later shown that there was little medium- to long-term effect on the performance of the firm.

Litigation finance

A perhaps unfamiliar option, here clients or the firm take funding from a third party to cover legal bills and costs of either their clients or of the firm itself. Funding is generally structured so that it is non-recourse, meaning that it does not encumber the balance sheets of law firms or their client. This method guarantees payments to firms in the short-term and may add a competitive edge in winning work today and for the future. There are few downsides for the law firm providing it ensures a reputable funder is introduced to its client or to its management board, to protect valuable relationships. Firms may seek to introduce such funding on a case-by-case basis or engage firm-wide on a portfolio of cases.

Law firm leaders are undoubtedly considering all the options available to them. Whilst familiar levers will initially rise to the top of the list, thought should be given to those that firms may yet to have fully engaged with. Litigation funding is likely to be one of these. With such funders in the UK having raised significant sums in recent years, support is likely to be available at both the speed and quantum that firms need to both shore up for today and ensure the firm is on a solid footing for tomorrow. When considering all the options for immediate cash needs, leaders should keep an eye on longer-term impact, in both financial and reputational terms.

Litigation finance as a risk-free option

Insurance for a huge variety of commercial risks has been commonplace for centuries. However, the historic principles of Champerty and Maintenance barred a third-party from funding legal cases in many jurisdictions and legal risks were not widely and legitimately transferrable until a few decades ago. Most governments, often with the assistance of the courts through case law that is supportive of third-party funding, have now adapted the rules in the name of enabling access to justice, and the litigation funding industry was born. Today, such funding is increasingly in demand from claimants and their lawyers, and by investors alike.

On the "demand side", claimants with legitimate commercial disputes can readily access third-party litigation funding. Such arrangements differ to traditional insurance policies in that, rather than requiring premiums to be paid in advance of the risk being taken on, no payment is required until a case is won or settled in favor of the claimant. Costs are in fact taken from winnings from the defendants. Should a case be lost, the funder takes the loss without recourse to the claimant, who has no costs to pay. It is worth noting that even in the event of a winning claim, if there is insufficient recovery from the defendant to meet the funding party's costs, the insured will not be liable to the funding party.

Such a risk transfer mechanism can be appealing to claimants in a variety of situations. Many legal disputes are unexpected, so those without legal budgets set aside for litigation can often find third-party funding attractive. So too can those businesses without the significant free cash flow required for funding of often hefty legal fees. That said, funding is increasingly attractive also to cash-rich organizations that wish to manage their working capital and to transfer risks of litigation, turning a potential sizable liability into an asset.

Well-managed funders have effective case management processes in place. Often combining analytical and legal skill, they assess cases on a variety of bases including naturally the legal merits, but also the financial dynamics of the claim, the defendant's ability to pay, and the lawyer's caliber. Such processes act as a filter, often leading to only two to three percent of cases offered to funders being taken on. This ensures the funders a high success rate, often above 70 percent, as is the case with Augusta. The result is strong returns on capital that have not gone unnoticed on the "supply-side" amongst institutional investors.

In today's low yield highly volatile markets, many sophisticated investors are seeking innovative asset classes to diversify their portfolios. Money has flowed in increasing quantum into the litigation funding industry over the past several years, as savvy pension and credit funds seek to access this emerging asset class. Augusta Ventures, for example, raised £150m in 2018 and a further £135m in 2019 from significant institutions. Offers of additional capital are a regular event and seem set to increase given continuing macroeconomic uncertainty, in part accentuated by the worrying advent of the Coronavirus, which has highlighted the uncorrelated nature of the asset class.

The challenge for funders is to manage risk in their portfolios. It is all too easy for ambitious individuals with an understanding of litigation to seek to pile into the industry. From experience, it takes time to build effective risk management processes and to identify optimal segments of the market. The key is to select case types, jurisdictions, and law firms that offer rational, predictable behaviors and outcomes. In much the same way as a commercial insurer relies on past policy data, legal track records need to be analyzed and modelled to understand potential risks and returns for each new claim opportunity.

With hype around the industry growing, both investors seeking to place capital in litigation funders and claimants looking for funding for their cases should carefully consider the appropriate funder to work with. Those participating in the UK-based self-regulatory body ALF – the Association of Litigation Funders – promise to act transparently, fairly, and to ensure appropriate returns for claimants. ALF membership demonstrates a commitment to good governance and fair businesses practices akin to established insurers. Given the low barriers to entry in the industry, it is feasible that poorly managed and undercapitalized litigation funders may be set up. ALF exists to assure both investors and claimants that its members are trustworthy counterparties.

In a little under a decade, litigation funding has gone from a novel phenomenon to a must-have for sophisticated litigation lawyers and their clients. Studies indicate that 80 percent of lawyers expect the funding industry to grow apace into 2021.[1] This trend on the demand side will only cement appetite on the supply side amongst investors. The challenge for those wishing to access the strong returns that are uncorrelated to traditional asset classes is access to proven managers with demonstrable track records and processes. This will remain the case for some time given the timescale that it takes a manager to build and implement systems, and then prove its ability to effectively deploy and recover capital. Those litigation funds set up with the proper processes offer both claimants and investors insurance-like returns and risk transfer. These are attractive in today's uncertain environment and promise to widen access to justice, which is undoubtedly a social good.

The mechanics of litigation finance

Litigation funding solution

The advance of litigation funding over the past decade changes the dynamic by providing a win-win solution for law firms and their clients. It does this by enhancing the value of the counter-cyclical hedge through increasing the quantity of litigation and the quality of law firm revenue.

Litigation funding is not only the preserve of class actions. Augusta's experience in the UK is that most standard funded claims (litigation and arbitration) involve commercial disputes. The majority of those include business-to-business claims for breach of contract, professional negligence, and shareholder disputes.

How litigation funding can help

With litigation funding, the funder pays for legal costs, counsel fees, and disbursements. A major attraction of litigation funding is that it is non-recourse, whereby if the case loses, the funded party pays nothing. The funder generally meets the law firm's costs and claim-associated expenses, and the claim holder can also cover the adverse cost risk (the loser pays the other side's costs) through after-the-event insurance (ATE). In return, the funder charges a commission based on either a multiple of funds invested in the case or percentage of damages awarded upon a successful resolution. Depending on the ratio of costs to damages, the claimant would generally expect to receive around 70-80 percent of the damages, though this is reliant upon the proportionality between the claim size and cost to run.

With funding, businesses can pursue meritorious claims while benefiting from:

- Increased liquidity – cash is retained to meet immediate business needs as opposed to paying legal fees;
- Positive P&L impact – funding keeps ongoing litigation costs off a business' profit and loss as the expense is borne by the funder;
- Risk mitigation – the risk of adverse cost can be covered by a funder indemnity or funded ATE insurance policy, resulting in avoiding having to report a contingent liability on the balance sheet;
- Claim expertise – the funder acts as a project manager, collaborating with the law firm so reducing management time;
- Independent claim diligence – the work the funder undertakes provides assurance on the strength of their case as a funder's legal team undertakes thorough due diligence prior to funding to ensure the claim has merit; and
- Control – at all times the claim owner retains control of the litigation.

Financing also means that law firms can attract more opportunities that benefit their relationship with their clients by introducing the option of non-recourse litigation funding. The funder is aligned with the business as they want a positive outcome and would prefer to spend more on good advice, where required, to achieve a successful resolution. The law firm avoids potential client conflict over billing, as the funder deals with invoices based on pre-agreed budgets. The result is that the quantity of work for law firms should grow to offset falling advisory revenue and the quality of work is attractive as law firms are not forced into aggressive fee caps or fee deferrals. The use of funding shifts the risk from the business and law firm to the funder.

Without funding, the alternative is a lose-lose. Businesses fail to exploit and monetize good meritorious claims and law firms are left with litigation resources being potentially underutilized. Let litigation funding help you access valuable and scarce cash in these challenging times.

Commercial models for utilizing litigation financing

As outlined above, litigation funding provides a mechanism for balancing litigation risk between a claimant, law firm, and funder. There are various commercial structures available to achieve this objective and it is important that all parties seek to ensure that risk is balanced as efficiently as possible. Outlined below are the key features of the three typical models of litigation finance.

Model one – single case funding

Under a single case structure, a funder provides a facility to a claimant to pay the cost of conducting a single dispute. The facility amount is determined based on an agreed budget and the facility is drawn down each month by the claimant to pay approved invoices submitted by their legal team.

If the case is successful, the funder's investment and success fee is repaid in priority from the proceeds of the successful resolution and, if the case is lost, the funder's investment is lost. The terms of the funder's success fee will vary depending on the risk profile of the individual case; however, the success fee is commonly equal to either (or a hybrid) of:

- A multiple of the amount of funds drawn from the facility at the date of resolution; or
- A percentage of the gross proceeds received from the respondent.

In considering the commercial dynamic of single case funding, it is important to note that this model exposes the funder's investment to a simple and relatively binary outcome (the case is either won or lost) and the funder's success fee will reflect this risk.

Model two – portfolio funding

Under a portfolio arrangement, a funder pays the cost of conducting multiple cases through a single facility. This model creates an efficient solution for clients seeking to pursue several claims simultaneously – for example, clients with multiple cases across an entire business or a discrete set of claims relating to a particular project.

The defining feature of a portfolio arrangement is that the funder's investment is "cross-collateralized" across all the cases included in the facility. Unlike a single case investment where the outcome is binary, the funder's risk is now spread across the outcomes of multiple cases and the funder is repaid from the cases that resolve successfully. This dynamic can substantially lower the risk profile of the funder's investment which, most relevantly from the client's perspective, should result in a lower success fee than funding on a single case basis.

In addition to enhancing flexibility in relation to the commercial terms of funding, depending on the size and composition of the portfolio, cross-collateralization also allows funders and clients to consider options to streamline the standard of diligence required for a case to be approved for investment.

The emergence of portfolio funding has allowed the funding industry to efficiently cater to the commercial needs of sophisticated clients by providing a more strategic "business-wide" solution to their litigation expenditure. Consistent with this commercial approach, depending on the preference of the claimants, funders may also consider including in the facility an amount of working capital finance to be used to support the business of the claimant.

Model three – law firm funding

The two models outlined above contemplate funders providing finance to claimants directly. As a rapidly growing alternative, funders are increasingly providing finance directly to law firms. These facilities are structured to enable law firms to draw on funding to underwrite their operating costs while acting for their clients on a contingency basis. The funding to the firm is still characterized as "non-recourse" as the finance is repaid by the firm from the proceeds of the firm's realized contingent work. The client simply retains their share of the proceeds based on the terms of their contingency arrangement with the firm.

Depending on the terms of the facility and the amount charged by the funder, the law firm will retain a material share of the contingent proceeds upon success, which provides potential for significant upside to the firm while protecting against cashflow pressure and downside risk in the event the case is unsuccessful. In addition to the potential financial return to the firms, balancing risk through a facility can provide law firms with the strategic opportunity to satisfy client demand and grow their practice by acting on a contingency basis.

Conclusion

Proactive cash flow management is critical to the success of any law firm. The cash position of most firms has been refined over time to enhance partner distributions and to manage cash balances as efficiently as possible. This traditional strategy has been challenged by COVID-19. Firms must consider all aspects of their business to determine the financing options most suited to both balancing risk and growing their practices.

Reference

1 Burford: 2020 Legal Finance Report: A survey of in-house and law firm lawyers. www.burfordcapital.com

Chapter 7:
A flexible financial future

Andy Poole, legal sector partner, Armstrong Watson

Although it has never been easy to run a successful law firm, I generally advise firms to keep their financial management simple. As people businesses, the key historically for law firms has been to keep their people busy; to quickly raise invoices based on how busy their people are; and to speedily receive payment for those invoices. Law firms that have got those three things right have tended to out-perform their rivals.

As we move beyond COVID-19, law firm management may no longer be so simple, and future law firm leaders will need to be far more flexible.

How law firms have historically managed their practices and finances

Although practice management has modernized during the past ten to 20 years, the basics have generally remained the same for generations.

Fee earners have been employed by practices, and those fee earners have been provided with fee generation targets based on their hours of production, which has been office-based. As fee-earners have become busier, additional fee earners have been recruited. If firms have had more than one office, duplicate fee earners have been employed in each office, even where each individual fee earner has not necessarily been fully utilized.

Those fee earners have been directly supported by employed secretaries, typists, receptionists, IT personnel, marketing personnel, finance personnel, HR personnel etc. Fees have been based on the time spent on client affairs, either directly or as an indirect check of efficiency where market expectations are for fixed fees for certain work-types.

Fee earner salaries have been partly based on individual billing levels, with many firms setting ratios of fees raised to salary rewards, and with bonuses being based on individual billing. The fee earners that have been more successful at production and billing have generally been promoted to become partners, department heads, to the management board, or to become a managing partner.

There has been a certain mystique and attraction of promotion to become a partner, and a perception (mostly internally) of the importance of that title.

Firms have had a large number of partners relative to the size of a business, due to a wish to retain good fee earners, as well as the need for additional capital to be provided to the firm by the partners as a result of a focus on billing rather than cash collection.

Partners have typically been rewarded either as a fixed share for salaried partners/fixed share equity; or as equal full equity or lockstep to equal full equity based on time-served.

Practices have been collegiate, with an emphasis on collective management decisions even where there is a management board. Management boards and department heads have not actively managed the performance of partners, and many partners have not been prepared to be managed.

Firms have focused on profit per equity partner, year by year, especially with changing profit-sharing ratios and changes in partners. Short-term financial management rather than long-term planning has therefore resulted.

Case management systems and paper-lite electronic document management systems have eased legal processes, but have not revolutionized them – the IT packages have been based on the same processes being carried out, just in a more streamlined and quicker way.

The legal sector market has been dominated by a large number of small firms – certainly this is the case in the UK. According to the SRA's *The changing legal services market report*,[1] there are just over 10,000 law firms in England and Wales, with around half of those having annual fees lower than £400,000.

It is understandable why law firms have been managed in the way they have. In the Law Society's Financial Stability Toolkit,[2] which I co-authored with Peter Scott, I outlined the drivers of profitability and cashflow.

There we discussed how profits are influenced more by boosting top line income than by reducing overheads, since there are only so many cuts you can make to expenditure before you're not able to operate effectively. We also covered the basics of fee generation being based on utilization and recovery – in effect, having busy fee earners record their matter-related time (utilization) and then raising bills to cover that matter-related time at the fee earner's charge out rate (recovery). The higher the utilization and recovery, the higher the fees will be and the higher the profits should be.

We also covered the concepts of WIP days (the time taken between undertaking the work and raising a bill) and Debtor days (the time between raising a bill and it being paid) as the main drivers of cash flow.

The historic practices summarized above have worked well for lots of law firms over many years, and although there is an argument for saying "if it ain't broke, don't fix it", in recent times pressure has been growing on some of the approaches, which have slowly evolved as a result. COVID-19 hit like a thunderbolt in 2020 and that gradual change was replaced by a seismic shift, revolutionizing the future management of law firms.

The impact of COVID-19 on the performance and finances of law firms

When the first lockdown of 2020 occurred in March 2020, law firms first reacted with shock and then a steely determination to be able to continue to operate. It was remarkable how quickly IT systems were established to allow people to continue working – including video conferencing facilities, remote connectivity, electronic document management systems and so on. Within a very short time period, people became comfortable with new ways of working and although there has been a little Zoom/Teams fatigue, clients and all the people within law firms tend now to be quite happy using technology to interact rather than having to travel for meetings – and that is here to stay.

In the early days of the pandemic, fee income was initially reduced as a result of:

- House completions not being permitted other than in specific circumstances;
- Reduced demand due to market uncertainty;
- Slowed initial production;
- Closure of Courts; and
- Slowing of responses/involvement from others in the legal process.

In many areas, demand and fees increased hugely from July onwards as property transactions boomed and people realized COVID-19 was here to stay for a while and they therefore "needed to get on with it".

Firms benefited from cash and overhead savings in a number of ways, including:

- Staff furlough scheme;
- CBILS and Bounce Back loans;

- VAT and other tax deferrals;
- Vastly reduced printing and postage;
- Vastly reduced travel; and
- Vastly reduced training and marketing events.

As a result, at the end of 2020 most firms were in a better financial position than they had been for a very long time, with profits and cash-flow much higher than expected even on slightly lower year-to-date fee income. Many found that they were able to operate with reduced headcount, either with fee earners being able to work without as much support or because furloughing fee earners had demonstrated that not as many lawyers were actually required for the level of activity.[3]

Before the pandemic, many law firms and people within firms had been reluctant to change, providing a plethora of arguments for why they could not have people working from home; why they needed to have hard copy documents; why they needed to print; why they needed to post; why they needed to meet people face-to-face. Suddenly due to COVID-19, they were unable to do those things. They were forced to accept the change, and they realized it wasn't only possible, but the change wasn't so bad after all, and was mostly beneficial for all parties.

That said, one area where law firms have struggled when working remotely is looking after and developing their people. Significant longer-term negative impacts on practices are the likely result when it is more difficult to induct new joiners, train trainees, supervise staff, provide suitable working environments, protect from mental health issues, develop ideas, or maintain a firm-wide culture. These negative impacts may well outweigh the positive financial benefits that a COVID-19 forced change of approach has created.

The positive financial results may have also, in part, been influenced by those people not on furlough working longer hours, fearful for their future and covering for those on furlough. Although firms may be more profitable on the face of it, there may be a "human" cost behind that profit. Such costs may not be sustainable and fee earner/owner fatigue is being experienced, adding to mental health concerns.

Anticipated impacts on law firms as we emerge from COVID-19

Savvy law firm leaders have been quick to take advantage of the mind-set change of their people. A big part of the battle of changing anything in an organization, is acceptance of the change by the people within it. COVID-19 provided the perfect opportunity – the association of why change is required and the acknowledgement that the perceived negative impacts of change weren't as expected.

By the above, I don't simply mean that because the short-term financial results have been positive that law firm leaders should continue to operate in the same way as they have during COVID-19. Some people may want to continue to work the way they have been forced to, whilst others may want to go straight back to the office. It is not a straight choice between the two.

Given the potential people development issues noted earlier, it would not be the right course of action to simply force people to continue to work remotely, however tempting potential rent savings may be if large office environments could be left behind. Offices are therefore likely to stay, but potentially not quite as we've seen them before.

For those returning to the office, many may be tempted to go back to operating in pre-COVID-19 ways. People became used to operating in a particular way when they were last in the office and there is a danger that they will revert to type when returning to that environment. When working remotely people can understand why they are not able to print/post/meet as easily, but when back in an office environment with printers close by there is a risk of reverting to old behaviors.

It should not be a straight choice of working remotely with the people risks but (potentially short-term) financial benefits versus working in offices with the people benefits but financial costs. It's much more likely that for those who need to work in the office (such as those benefiting from interaction to avoid mental health issues, or those who don't have comfortable home working conditions) will return full-time to the office, and others will alternate between working remotely and working in the office.

Those law firms that effectively change their systems and processes to lock-in the forced benefits of COVID-19 will out-perform those that do not. Remaining paperless/paper-lite with reduced postage and reduced travel will result in more efficient use of time and lower expenditure.

Of course, it's not *just* about post and print and travel. It's the whole end-to-end process that should be reviewed. As firms emerge from COVID-19 there is a perfect opportunity for people to understand and acknowledge that change is required and is beneficial. Those firms that undertake lean process management reviews will reap the benefits. Those that make the same mistake as case management implementation in just replicating what was already done, but a little more efficiently, will not. Challenge is required step-by-step on what is done, by whom, at what stage, what further technology/AI can be used, how the information flow will work etc. The processes should be amended and documented and controls implemented to ensure they are followed.

Such longer-term thought and planning will be necessary given that some of the profit and cashflow benefits that law firms enjoyed in 2020 are time-limited. The property transactions boom has partially been based on a stamp duty exemption, pent-up demand and lifestyle change choices. Furlough, loans, and tax deferrals will also cease. Wider economic factors will also impact law firms. Through recession, demand may reduce in some areas such as corporate transactions but increase in others such as insolvency and potentially litigation. We are likely to find peaks and troughs in a number of departments within law firms, with those peaks and troughs most likely at different times for each. That bumpy road will make law firm management much more difficult – making swift decisions when demand falters and appropriate staffing and cash flow planning decisions when demand increases. Even in the positive of increased demand, there are risks of over-trading where long lock up means that cash income falls behind cash outflows.

For the above reasons, there are risks that a number of law firms may become insolvent or realize that they cannot continue. Some may conclude that law firm mergers will be the result, and there may well be increased merger activity to a certain extent – but there is also a risk that the firms will simply fall over and others will pick up the pieces (staff and clients) without having to go through a formal merger/acquisition process. Either way, such consolidation is likely to finally reduce the total number of law firms, especially as individuals that may look to start up on their own are now more likely to join a virtual/platform firm instead.

A smaller amount of larger firms are also likely to be better placed to continue to have the resources to ensure compliance, reduce risk, and invest in future technology.

Lessons learned from the COVID-19 experience

Many lessons have been learned from the COVID-19 experience. In good times, it tends not to be quite so important whether all guns are firing as effectively as they can be, since positive results still tend to follow. In more troubled times, much more focus needs to be applied, and effective approaches need to be introduced and then become habitual. The most relevant lessons will differ for each firm, but are likely to include the following.

Cash is king, and businesses fail due to a lack of cash, not necessarily a lack of profit. Being prudent is important, but cash *flow* is more important. Work in progress (WIP) and debtors need to be as low as possible in order to convert work into cash.

Work may need to be turned down if it is not profitable or the team is too busy – taking on too much work will put the team under strain, potentially mean that mistakes are made, and result in a cash drain.

Pricing should be used more actively to manage peaks and troughs in demand – making hay while the sun shines and increasing demand when it does not.

Increased risk may mean that fewer fee earners want to take on the risk of becoming partners – it is not the holy grail it once was.

If WIP and debtors are reduced, not as many partners may be required to fund working capital anyway, thus resulting in higher profits per partner.

Although annual profits are important, longer-term focus is required to ensure the success of firms. Looking to be able to invest and build capital value may be more appropriate than viewing legal practices as annual income generation vehicles.

Firms need to be able to make decisions quickly, not by partnership consensus.

Postage and printing is not required in the volumes that it was pre-COVID-19. Large-scale marketing events don't necessarily provide a return on investment – many firms have found that online marketing has been more effective and cheaper. Not all staff always need to work standard hours from 9am to 5pm. Clients are happy to use technology and have become accustomed to video conferencing. Travel costs and time can therefore be saved. Working remotely can work well.

Services can be provided over a wider geographical area – the use, and acceptance, of video conferencing has levelled the playing field for many.

Reliance on large and costly offices can be reduced but not removed entirely. Offices of the future may not need to be as large as they once were – if not all people are working in the office at the same time, office hot desking will be more financially effective and so offices will need to be set up and equipped in a way that allows for that.

Not as many staff may be required. A number of law firms have undertaken redundancy programs after COVID-19, proving that they were carrying too many people for the level of activity, even pre-COVID-19.

If there are to be peaks and troughs in activity, firms with large set overheads may struggle to cover them all of the time. In order to reduce set overheads, a variety of tactics can be used, including outsourcing, off-shoring, and north-shoring. Consolidation will allow fee earners to concentrate on fee earning, management to concentrate on management, and more resources to be available for investment.

Law firms of the future

It is important not to throw the baby out with the bath water – the basics still apply. Profits are fees less overheads and the main overhead as a people business will still be the people costs. Therefore, knowing and then covering the costs of production (salaries) will still be important. The fundamentals of profit and cash generation discussed above will therefore remain vital, albeit with a more flexible approach.

There is likely to be a continued rise of the virtual/platform fee sharing firms. Such vehicles will be increasingly attractive for those that have enjoyed the flexibility of working from home, have a following, do not want to be part of the politics of a larger professional partnership, and are driven by direct rewards linked to their fee generation.

Beyond those virtual/platform firms (that will become larger in any event as noted above), general practices are likely to become larger themselves either via mergers/acquisitions or by taking on additional staff and clients from failed firms. The larger scale will allow them to invest in technology and their long-term future.

The larger firms are likely to have lower numbers of equity partners compared to the size of the business. Although this may permit higher profits per partner, this will allow an approach to be developed to maximize long-term capital with a view to having trade sale exits. If this is to succeed, systems and processes will become ever-more important in order to reduce reliance on key people, maximize efficiencies and profit generation and to reduce lock-up so that pressure is not placed on working capital requirements.

Fewer equity owners will make it easier to have effective and streamlined people management and decision making. This will be vital if law firm leaders are to be nimble enough to cope with the peaks and troughs that are to come and allow the flexible management that will be required. It will also allow for law firms to be managed by professional business managers, and so managing partners may continue to be replaced by non-lawyer chief executives and for the board to be made up of finance, HR, and IT professionals.

The need for flexible management is likely to include having a mix of remote and office working, more regular changes in the required workforce, new technology and changing lean processes, and not always having all back office support provided in-house.

Much of this flexibility will change law firms from having a larger number of fixed overheads to more variable costs. Traditionally, law firms have high fixed costs for salaries, rent and professional indemnity insurance. If demand reduces it is more difficult to reduce fixed costs without draconian redundancy programs or cutting hours of all staff. If the costs were already variable, then they would automatically fall with reductions in demand.

Some of this will be achieved via outsourcing – and this should not necessarily just include back-office costs such as secretaries, typists, or receptionists. This can include IT/IT director/finance director level support and it can include fee earners too. Outsourcing fee earners has already started with the larger firms, where work is "north-shored" to offices/firms in cheaper locations or "off-shored" to offices/firms overseas. Some of the larger firms have started to formally launch separately branded more flexible services. Vario from Pinsent Masons for example – meaning variety/difference in Latin – is intended to provide more flexible solutions to the company's clients. Freelance legal professionals are used in such situations that may not necessarily be employed full-time by the law firm, and may be rewarded matter by matter. This matches the concept of the virtual/platform firms, providing increased flexibility to the client, to the fee earner, and to the law firm. Such flexible approaches will help to reduce costs and to protect against peaks and troughs in demand.

As the workforce requirements change, so will reward, and we may find that reward becomes more performance based. Although some of the virtual/platform-based initiatives may reward people based on a percentage of their fees, by solely incentivizing on fees there is a danger that it will result in the wrong behaviors such as clients being hoarded and important factors such as client care and cashflow being forgotten about. Reward packages are therefore more likely to be flexible and based on a balanced scorecard approach. In order to get the best out of partners as well as staff, and to attract the best people, the concept of performance-based partner profit share is therefore likely to continue to expand too.

As reward changes and becomes more flexible, so too must law firm pricing. Clients are increasingly demanding choice and a move away from hourly rates to fixed fees or value-based fees. In fact, there are around 20 different ways to price legal services and it will become more important to think case by case about which of the pricing options should be offered to clients. Although law firms may still continue to monitor recoveries as an efficiency measure, hourly rates are less likely to be used as the basis for fees, and a more flexible pricing approach will be needed, including varying charges even month-by-month based on demand.

In conclusion, the buzzword of the future of law firm management will be *flexible*. Flexible working locations, flexible working hours, flexible office environments, flexible staffing, flexible reward, flexible back office support, flexible processes, and flexible pricing.

All of that will take more time and focus from the management team and so the structure of management will need to become more business-like, with management working "on" the business rather than "in" the business.

References

1 SRA – *The Changing Legal Services Market*: changing-legal-services-market.pdf
2 The Law Society – Financial Stability Toolkit: Financial Stability Toolkit – Law Society Bookshop
3 Armstrong Watson: *The Impact of COVID-19 on the Legal Sector* https://www.armstrongwatson.co.uk/services/covid-19-and-your-business/impact-covid-19-legal-sector

www.ingramcontent.com/pod-product-compliance
Ingram Content Group UK Ltd.
Pitfield, Milton Keynes, MK11 3LW, UK
UKHW021848150926
8657IPUK00005B/136

9 781783 584048